Reteaching Math
ALGEBRA READINESS

Mini-Lessons, Games & Activities to Review
& Reinforce Essential Math Concepts & Skills

Jeff Grabell & Bob Krech

New York • Toronto • London • Auckland • Sydney
Mexico City • New Delhi • Hong Kong • Buenos Aires

Teaching *Resources*

DEDICATION

For Kris, Adam, Ben, and Erica
—J.G.

ACKNOWLEDGMENTS

Mandy, "The Math Dog," for all her help with my math program;
Tom Sexton, for showing me how to make it inviting;
and Nishi Metha, for teaching me that "factories make products."
—J.G.

Editor: Maria L. Chang
Cover design by Brian LaRossa
Interior design by Holly Grundon
Interior illustrations by Mike Moran

ISBN-13: 978-0-439-52966-2
ISBN-10: 0-439-52966-2

1 2 3 4 5 6 7 8 9 10   40   15 14 13 12 11 10 09 08

Table of Contents

Table of Contents (continued)

Introduction

Most math books that have the word *reteaching* in the title typically feature many pages of equations and practice problems. The reasoning may be that if students require a concept or skill to be retaught, the best way for them to gain mastery is to practice more of the same. Research does show that some students need more time on a task than others in order to learn a concept. However, if a student does not understand a concept or skill the first time, presenting a series of problems that the student already finds difficult and repeating them, without new knowledge or intervention, will most likely not be successful.

To reteach implies actually teaching again, not merely repeated practice. Students need to have a strong conceptual understanding if they are going to be able to do mathematics with accuracy and comprehension. Without this understanding, math can become meaningless, and students simply work by rote. That's why we've created the Reteaching Math series. You will find this series is different from most reteaching books in that the emphasis is on helping students develop understanding as well as on providing useful practice.

Using a Problem-Solving Approach

The activities, games, and lessons in this book are just plain good instruction, with an emphasis on solving problems and applying math in context. Problem solving is the first process standard listed in the NCTM *Principles and Standards for School Mathematics* (2000). The accompanying statement reads, "Problem solving should be the central focus of all mathematics instruction and an integral part of all mathematical activity." In other words, problem solving is what math is all about. Every lesson here begins with a problem to solve to help create a spirit of inquiry and interest. Practice problems are integrated into the lessons so they are meaningful. Real reteaching!

Providing Context

It is important to provide students with a context to help give learning mathematical skills and concepts meaning. Context helps learners understand how these mathematical ideas and tools are useful and can be applied to real-life problems and situations. Context can be provided by creating a theme that carries throughout all the lessons. In this book, the theme of Professor Percy Palindrome's Secret Laboratory provides a context in which learning about algebra is relevant, motivating, and fun. A generous dose of humor is included to help ease the anxiety many students feel over algebra in particular, and math in general. The use

Teaching Tip

....

Math Journal/Notebook

Have students keep their math notes, practice papers, and other work in a math journal/notebook. This can be a simple three-ring binder with some blank lined paper. Throughout this book you will find journal prompts that will help your students solidify their understanding of concepts by writing explanations about the ideas in their own words. As they do this, students will be creating their own personal math reference book. The practice pages, which include a Basics Box, should be kept in the journal as well so students will be able to refer back to previous work to help them with definitions, skills, concepts, and ideas.

of the overarching laboratory theme gives all the lessons a sense of cohesion, purpose, and interest.

Addressing Various Learning Styles

A good way to help all students learn mathematics well is to present ideas through physical, pictorial, and symbolic representations. Research suggests the importance of learning math ideas through modeling with manipulatives. Math concepts need to be experienced on a physical level before pictorial and more abstract representations can be truly understood. Relying completely on symbolic representations (e.g., lots of equations) is rarely enough, particularly in a reteaching situation.

Learning experiences featured here include using manipulatives, drawing pictures, writing equations, reading stories, and playing games to help learners gain a strong conceptual knowledge.

What's Inside?

Activity Lessons – introduce major concepts and skills. Timed to last about 40 minutes, these lessons are designed to help students work on the ideas in a hands-on manner and context to help them understand the meaning behind the math and give them an opportunity to apply it in a fun way.

Practice Pages – are specially designed to provide both practice and a helpful reference sheet for students. Each practice page begins with a **word problem** so students can see how and why the math is useful in solving real problems. Each page also features a **Basics Box**. Here, concepts are carefully presented with words, numbers, pictures, definitions, and step-by-step explanations. **Example problems** help solidify understanding, then a series of problems give students meaningful practice. Finally, a **journal prompt** helps students discuss and explore the concept using pictures, numbers, and words, while providing you an assessment opportunity that looks at student thinking and understanding. Practice pages can be worked on together in class, assigned to be done independently, or given as homework assignments.

Review Pages – provide students with additional focused practice on a specific math concept. The concept is practiced in a variety of formats and is designed to be completed independently. In addition, a **mixed review** of concepts introduced earlier is included in many review pages. By spiraling the curriculum in this way, students' retention and recall of math ideas is supported. These pages may be used for review, practice, homework, or assessment of students' knowledge and understanding.

How to Use This Book

This book can be used as a replacement unit, as a resource for activities for math workshops or centers, or as a supplement to find engaging ideas to enhance a textbook unit. The lessons and activities are presented in a developmental sequence, but can be used as stand-alone or supplementary learning experiences. Since it's written to accommodate all learners, you can use it to teach algebra readiness to any class.

About Multiplication and Division

Algebra is listed by the NCTM as one of the five main content strands in mathematics, however its significance cuts across all strands. The methods and ideas learned in algebra support a wide variety of mathematics. Algebra focuses on looking for relationships and patterns, ways of representing mathematical ideas, and analyzing. All of these ideas are useful in solving many types of problems. And that's what mathematics is all about—using ideas and tools to solve problems. Algebra is a tool to do just that.

The NCTM Standards for algebra include the following expectations for grades 4–6:

All students should:

- Describe, extend, and make generalizations about geometric and numeric patterns
- Represent and analyze patterns and functions, using words, tables, and graphs
- Identify such properties as the commutative, associative, and distributive properties and use them to compute with whole numbers
- Represent the idea of a variable as an unknown quantity using a letter or a symbol
- Express mathematical relationships using equations
- Model problem situations with objects and use representations such as graphs, tables, and equations to draw conclusions
- Investigate how a change in one variable relates to a change in a second variable
- Identify and describe situations with constant or varying rates of change and compare them

In addition, key ideas addressed in this book include:

- Patterns can be classified as either repeating (recurring) or growing (sequential). It is possible to identify patterns and extend them.
- Mathematical situations can be represented in a variety of ways.
- Symbols help us make mathematical generalizations.
- Equations show the relationship between two amounts. The equal sign is a symbol that means "the same as," not "the answer to the problem is."
- A function is one type of equation in which elements of one set of numbers are associated with elements of another set of numbers.

Part 1: Patterns

Materials

- Letter #1 (p. 30)
- transparency of Letter #1
- overhead marker
- pattern blocks
- Practice Page #1 (p. 31)
- Review Page #1 (p. 32)
- pencil

Teaching Tip

Algebra Word Wall

As students work through this unit, they'll encounter several new vocabulary words. Keep a list of this algebra vocabulary on a word wall bulletin board or chart. This word wall should have each word written clearly with an accompanying example and picture or diagram. You may want to assign pairs of students to draw and label certain terms for the chart. This can serve as a classroom reference that grows. As words are added to the class chart, have students add them to a similar chart in their math journals. By the end of this lesson, you should have the following words in your word wall: *pattern, recurring pattern, element,* and *core.*

Professor Palindrome Attempts to Contact the Aliens
(RECURRING PATTERNS)

Overview: Students are introduced to the idea of recurring patterns and the terms *element* and *core*.

Announce to the class: "I have received a rather peculiar letter that I would like to share with you." Pass out copies of the letter from Professor Palindrome to students. Give them a few minutes to read the letter silently, then invite students to take turns reading it aloud.

Focus on the first message Professor Palindrome sent to the aliens—the formula for toenail cleaner. It shows a sock, broccoli, and a fish, repeated several times. Ask: "What is the formula for toenail cleaner?" (*One sock, one broccoli, and one fish*)

Explain that the message to the aliens is a *pattern*—the formula repeated over and over. Patterns are made up of *elements*, which can include numbers, letters, and symbols. Ask students: "What are the elements in this pattern?" (*Sock, broccoli, and fish*) Place a transparency of the letter on the overhead and underline the sock, broccoli, and fish. Explain to students that these three items are the elements that make up the pattern. Tell them: "The part of a pattern that repeats over and over is called the *core*. The core is the smallest combination of elements that repeats in a pattern. A pattern that has a core that repeats over and over is called a *recurring pattern*." Write the terms *element, core,* and *recurring pattern* on the board.

Construct a similar pattern using pattern blocks, such as circle, square, trapezoid, circle, square, trapezoid, circle, square, trapezoid. Ask students: "How is the pattern I just made similar to Professor Palindrome's pattern?" (*Both patterns have three elements that repeat in the same sequence over and over*)

On the transparency, write *A* under the sock, *B* under the broccoli, and *C* under the fish. Tell the class: "Mathematicians often use letters as shortcuts to name a pattern. What letters are we using to name the elements in this message?" (*ABC*) "Does the pattern I made with the manipulatives follow an ABC pattern?" (*Yes*)

Have students work in pairs to find the gold-to-floss formula in the professor's second message. Ask: "What is the formula?" (*2 stalks of celery and 2 pieces of cheese*) "What are the elements in the message?" (*Celery and cheese*) "What is the core of the pattern?" (*Celery, celery, cheese, cheese*) Invite the class to call out the core of the pattern using letters. (*AABB*) Write the pattern on the board.

Follow the same procedure for the third message in the letter. In this case, the formula for raccoon mouthwash is wormy apple, crushed soda can, crushed soda can. Using letters, the core is ABB.

Tell students: "Now that you have had some practice identifying the core and elements of some of the professor's patterns, work with a partner to make some of your own." Provide each pair of students with some pattern blocks. Have partners take turns creating a pattern using the pattern blocks. The pattern should have at least three elements in the core. Then challenge the other partner to identify the core. Partners should take turns doing this twice. Circulate around the classroom and assist as needed. Then invite students to share a few sample patterns with the whole class to review the concepts of element, core, and recurring pattern.

ACTIVITY: The Pattern Museum

Put out a variety of manipulatives such as pattern blocks, interlocking cubes, and counting chips. Invite students to create their own pattern displays on their desks and write the core of their pattern on an index card, using letters (A, B, C) to identify the elements. As they set up their displays, make sure students turn their index cards upside down to hide their written pattern. When all displays are ready, have students move through the "museum" and identify and record the patterns they see on a sheet of paper. At the end of the class, have the pattern creators show the pattern on their index cards so everyone can check their answers.

Teaching Tip

Patterns All Around Us

Patterns are all around us. Phases of the moon, seasons of the year, and the day-night cycle are all naturally occurring patterns. The school schedule also follows a pattern. Invite students to help you create an ongoing, interactive bulletin board that features patterns they find at school and at home. They can either create something specifically for the bulletin board (such as a pattern created in art class) or bring in found items (such as a piece of wallpaper with a pattern).

As this collection grows, you may be able to use some of these artifacts as examples for concepts introduced throughout the unit of study. Recurring patterns, for example, can provide many opportunities to make connections to other areas of the curriculum, such as poetry (rhyme and meter patterns), science (water cycle, life cycle of plants), social studies (election cycles), art, music, and even physical education.

Materials

- Letter #2 (p. 33)
- Practice Page #2 (p. 34)
- Review Page #2 (p. 35)
- pencil

Literature Link

Six Dinner Sid by Inga Moore (Simon and Schuster, 1991)

Sid is a cat who lives at #1 Aristotle Street. He also lives at numbers 2, 3, 4, 5, and 6 Aristotle Street, but none of the neighbors on the street know this. Sid enjoys dinner every night at each house! The story follows Sid's patterns as he moves through his daily routines. This is a great book for jumping off into extensions about Sid. What if he were to get two meals at each house? What if he got one meal at #1, two meals at #2, and so on? Sid's story can be used to predict and extend plenty of patterns.

ACTIVITY LESSON #2

Hibbins Feeds the Flaboon

(EXTENDING AND PREDICTING PATTERNS)

Overview: By identifying the core of a pattern, students can practice extending and predicting the rest of the pattern.

Tell the class: "I have received yet another peculiar letter—this time from Professor Palindrome's assistant, Hibbins." Distribute copies of Letter #2 to students and read it aloud together.

Review the flaboon's feeding schedule and ask the class to identify the elements of the pattern. *(Avocado, beet, and cantaloupe)* Then ask students to identify the core, reminding them that the core is the smallest combination of elements that repeats in a pattern. *(Avocado, beet, cantaloupe, or ABC)* Ask: "What will the flaboon be fed on the 8th day? *(Beet)* If necessary, extend the ABC pattern one more time and count from 1 to 8, pointing to each element in its turn and stopping at beet. Then ask: "What food is on the feeding schedule for the 12th day?" *(Cantaloupe)* Again, if necessary, extend the core on the board two more times and count up to 12 until cantaloupe is reached.

Next, focus on Hibbins's chore schedule. Ask the class: "What is the core this time?" *(PBAA)* Then ask: "Can you predict the eleventh element or the chore on the eleventh day?" *(Align the atomic accordion)* Remind students that recurring patterns are made by repeating the core over and over again. Write PBAAPBAAPBAA on the board and ask the class to count to the 11th item. Repeat the process for day 16.

Teaching Tip

Multiples Shortcut

1	2	3	4	5	6	7	8	9	10	11	12
A	B	C	A	B	C	A	B	C	A	B	C

As students look at patterns and attempt to extend them, they often start out by writing the pattern until they reach the element in question. Help students begin to think about using multiples to find this same information more quickly. For example, in an ABCABC pattern, if we are asked to find the 12th element, it is not necessary to write out all 12 elements. When we examine this pattern with multiplication in mind, we see that each C is a multiple of 3. The 4th C would be 12, or 4 x 3.

ACTIVITY LESSON #3

The Aliens Respond

(*PATTERNS ON GRIDS*)

> Overview: Students learn that patterns can be arranged not only in a linear format, but also on grids.

Materials

- Letter #3 (p. 36)
- transparency of Letter #3
- overhead marker
- crayons
- graph paper
- Practice Page #3 (p. 37)
- Review Page #3 (p. 38)
- pencil

Tell the class: "We have received another strange letter, and guess from whom?" Pass out copies of Professor Palindrome's letter to students and read it aloud together.

Place a transparency of the letter on the overhead, and ask students: "What is the message?" (*Leave us alone*) Ask students to name the elements of the pattern (*leave, us, and alone*) and the core (*Leave us alone*). Remind students that in a recurring pattern, the core repeats over and over again. Call on volunteers to fill in the missing words from the message and complete the next line of the message. The completed grid should look like this:

Leave	Us	Alone	Leave	Us
Alone	Leave	Us	Alone	Leave
Us	Alone	Leave	Us	Alone
Leave	Us	Alone	Leave	Us
Alone	Leave	Us	Alone	Leave

The next line of the message would be:

Us	Alone	Leave	Us	Alone

Ask the class: "Where else have you seen patterns arranged in grids like this and not just in a straight line?" (*The calendar is perhaps the most common example, as well as number grids, such as a hundred chart.*) Explain to students that even though the pattern on a calendar or a hundred chart is an expanding pattern rather than a recurring one, it is clear that the pattern continues from the last element at the end of one row to the first element at the beginning of the next row. We can also see recurring patterns in such places as the tiles on walls and floors.

Using crayons and graph paper, have students create a 4-by-4 square grid that uses colors and symbols together to demonstrate a recurring pattern. When finished, invite students to share their grids and explain their patterns.

Literature Link

The Fly on the Ceiling
by Julie Glass
(Random House, 1998)

This engaging tale is based on one of math's greatest myths—the story about the father of analytic geometry, Rene Descartes, the mathematician who popularized the Cartesian system of coordinates. Did he really develop this idea because of a fly on his ceiling? Read the book and decide.

Materials

- Letter # 4 (p. 39)
- transparency of Letter #4
- overhead marker
- counters
- place-value blocks, toothpicks, and/or any other materials suitable for constructing three-dimensional sequences
- paper
- crayons/colored pencils
- Practice Page #4 (p. 40)
- Review Page #4 (p. 41)

ACTIVITY: **Gridlock Game**

Give a pair of students a deck of playing cards. Shuffle the deck and have players take turns picking a card from the deck, one at a time. The goal is to use the cards to form a repeating pattern, with players placing their picks in three rows of three cards for a total of nine cards. It could be a two- or three-element pattern based on suit, color, value, and any number of other attributes. If a player picks a card that doesn't fit the pattern, he or she can put it in a discard pile. When the picking pile is empty, shuffle the discard pile to put the cards back into play. The first player to complete the grid while keeping the pattern wins. For a greater challenge try it with a grid of 12 spaces.

ACTIVITY LESSON #4

The Cotton Candy Plants
(GROWING PATTERNS AND RULES)

> Overview: Students learn about growing patterns and how they can be described by using a rule.

Announce to the class that Professor Palindrome has sent another letter. Distribute copies of Letter #4 and read it aloud together.

Place a transparency of the letter on the overhead and direct students' attention to the growth chart for the Bulgarian cotton candy plant. Ask students: "What will the height of the plant be on the 7th day?" *(19")* "How did you figure out the height?" *(Add 3 to the prior day's height)* Draw brackets between two consecutive numbers on the growth chart (as shown below) and write the amount of change from one element to the next; in this case, +3.

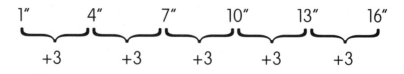

Explain to students that we can often find the pattern by looking at the relationship between the numbers. We can see that 4 is 3 more than 1, and that 7 is 3 more than 4, and that each subsequent number increases by 3. "Adding 3" to the previous element is the *rule* for this pattern. The *rule* describes how a pattern changes from one element to the next.

Ask students: "Using this rule, what would the height be on the 8th day?" (*22", because 19 + 3 = 22*) Have students work as partners to predict the height on the 25th day. (*73"*)

Next, focus on the growth chart for the Senegalese cotton candy plant. Ask students: "How tall with the plant be on the 7th day?" (*64"*) Invite students to justify their prediction and explain the rule. (*Take the prior day's height and double it or multiply by 2.*)

Demonstrate how the rule can be found by drawing brackets between two consecutive numbers on the growth chart and writing in the amount of change from one element to the next; in this case, ×2.

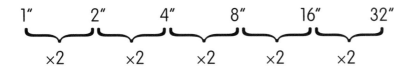

Challenge students to predict the plant's height on the 8th day (*128"*) and have them justify their answers. Ask the class how they would calculate the height on the 25th day. (*The pattern could be extended from the 8th day by doubling each prior day's height.*)

Ask the class: "How are these patterns different from the earlier patterns we received from Professor Palindrome?" (*The previous patterns were recurring patterns; these aren't.*) Explain to students that the patterns we are looking at now are called *growing patterns* or *sequences*. An example of a sequence is 2, 4, 6, 8, 10, 12. . . . In this case, the elements of the sequence increase by 2 each time. Recognizing that +2 is the rule for this pattern helps us identify the relationship between the numbers and determine that the relationship continues past the first two elements. For example, the sequence 2, 4, 8, 16, 32 . . . has the same first two elements as the first sequence, but the rule is to multiply by 2 each time, so it's important to always analyze the pattern beyond the first two elements.

Invite students to create their own growing pattern. Distribute crayons/colored pencils and/or three-dimensional materials to students. Ask them to create a sequence that extends for five elements. Have classmates predict the sixth element and explain the rule for the pattern. Share results either as a whole class or in small groups.

Literature Link

The King's Chessboard
by David Birch
(Penguin Puffin, 1988)

The king wants to reward a faithful wise man. At the king's insistence, the wise man replies, "I only ask this: Tomorrow, for the first square of your chessboard, give me one grain of rice; the next day, for the second square, two grains of rice . . . and so on for every square of the chessboard." The king agrees and soon learns a valuable lesson in mathematical patterns and humility.

ACTIVITY: **Well Paid**

After reading *The King's Chessboard* ask students if this concept of a doubling pattern could be applied to their own lives. What if they were paid one cent for the first day of doing a common household chore, such as washing the dishes, and that amount would be doubled every day for 10, 20, or even 30 days? Have students calculate their earnings based on this pattern. Using actual pennies and, eventually, calculators will help students understand the power of doubling.

—from *Meeting the Math Standards with Favorite Picture Books* by Bob Krech (Scholastic, 2002)

Materials

- Letter #5 (p. 42)
- transparency of Letter #5
- overhead marker
- Practice Page #5 (p. 44)
- Review Page #5 (p. 45)

ACTIVITY LESSON #5

Hibbins's Flops

(*START AND JUMP NUMBERS*)

> **Overview:** Students will learn how growing patterns have start and jump numbers.

Announce to the class: "It appears we have received another letter from Hibbins." Pair up students and distribute a copy of the letter to each student. Take turns reading it aloud.

Place the transparency of the letter on the overhead and point to the growth pattern of the first flop:

Day	Monday	Tuesday	Wednesday	Thursday
Weight (in grams)	2	5	8	11

Ask students: "How much do you think the flop will weigh on Friday and Saturday?" (*14 grams on Friday and 17 grams on Saturday*) "How do you know?" (*The rule for the pattern is to add 3 to the previous element.*) If necessary, draw brackets between two consecutive numbers to show that each number is 3 more than the previous one.

Repeat the process for the second flop:

Day	Monday	Tuesday	Wednesday	Thursday
Weight (in grams)	1	4	7	10

Ask students to compare the growth of the first and second flops. Students should identify that they both grow by 3 grams each day, but have different final weights. Discuss why. (*The first flop started out with a higher initial weight, so even though it gains 3 grams a day—the same as the second flop—it would eventually end up heavier.*)

Write the vocabulary words *start number* and *jump number* on the board. Explain that the start number is the first element of a pattern. The start number for the first flop was 2 while the start number for the second flop was 1. The jump number is the amount by which the pattern changes from one element to the next. Both flops had jump numbers of +3.

Thus far, most of the expanding patterns students have encountered have started with 1. Explain that in reality, most patterns do not begin with 1. Students are sure to be familiar with patterns like 2, 4, 6, 8 . . . and 10, 20, 30, 40 . . . , neither of which begins with 1.

ACTIVITY: **Hundred Chart Exploration**

To introduce the intriguing idea that sometimes patterns can be found within patterns, ask students if they notice another pattern in the weights of the two flops. (*The numbers alternate between odd and even numbers.*) Ask: "Why do you think this happens?" (*When you add an odd number to an even number, the sum is odd. When you add an odd number to an odd number, the sum is even.*) Divide the class into pairs and distribute the One Hundred Chart worksheet (p. 43). Challenge students to find different patterns using odd or even start numbers and odd or even jump numbers. They may discover that:

- an odd start number plus an even jump number equals an odd number

- an odd start number plus an odd jump number equals an even number

- an even start number plus an even jump number equals an even number

- an even start number plus an odd jump number equals an odd number

When students have finished, ask them to share their results with the class.

Literature Link

Anno's Magic Seeds
by Mitsumasa Anno
(Philomel, 1995)

A wizard gives Jack two golden seeds with special instructions. In the ensuing years, very interesting patterns develop as the seeds sprout and grow. Have students draw or diagram the events in this book and try to make predictions about what will happen next as the years pass for Jack. Full of complex counting and patterns, the story can make for some challenging questions and discussions.

ACTIVITY: **Start and Jump Game**

Give each pair of students a One Hundred Chart (p. 43), a die, a penny, and a dime. The first player rolls the die to determine his start number and places his coin on that number. He then rolls again to determine his jump number and then moves his coin accordingly. The next player does the same. Players take turns moving their coins across the One Hundred Chart based on the jump number they rolled. The first player to reach 100 wins.

Materials

- Letter #6 (p. 46)
- Function Machines (p. 47)
- Practice Page #6 (p. 50)
- Review Page #6 (p. 51)
- pencil

ACTIVITY LESSON #6

Dinner at the Lab

(FUNCTIONS AND FUNCTIONAL RELATIONSHIPS)

Overview: Students are introduced to the idea of a function—a relationship where elements of one set are associated with one or more elements of another set.

Inform the class that yet another letter has arrived from Hibbins. Distribute copies to students and read aloud together.

Ask students: "How might we help Hibbins determine the number of omelets, eggs, and pieces of toast he needs to prepare?" You might suggest beginning with the omelets. Since each guest will be served 1 omelet, 3 guests will require 3 omelets. Each omelet is made of 3 eggs so students can count by 3s to figure out how many eggs are needed. *(9 for 3 guests)* Challenge students to determine the number of pieces of toast for 3 guests, and then the quantities of omelets, eggs, and toast for 5 guests.

Ask students: "Can you think of a more efficient way to arrive at the answers?" Explain that by writing this information in a table or chart, the relationships between the numbers can be seen more clearly and multiplication as a strategy may emerge. On the board, draw the chart on page 17.

Number of guests	1	2	3	4	5
Number of omelets	1	2	3	4	5
Number of eggs	3	6	9	12	15
Number of toast pieces	2	4	6	8	10

Tell students, "What we are looking for is a function." Write the word *function* on the board and explain that a function is a relation where elements of one set are associated with one or more elements of another set. A function can also be defined as a relation where one thing is dependent on another. For example, the number of eggs needed depends on the number of omelets ordered. For every omelet, you need 3 eggs. So in this case, the function is "times 3."

Explain to students that sometimes we demonstrate these relationships using Function Machines. Draw a simple function machine on the board. Say, "For example, let's say I put a 4 in a function machine and a 7 comes out. Then I put a 2 in and a 5 comes out. Finally, I put a 10 in and a 13 comes out. What is the function?" (*Add 3*)

Pair up students and give each student a copy of the Function Machines sheet (p. 47). Have students decide on a function for each machine (for example, minus 2), then fill in the input and output numbers on each machine. Remind students that a function applies to all the numbers in each machine. When students are finished, have them trade papers with their partners to see if they can determine the functions of each machine. When these are completed, invite students to share some examples with the class and see if they can determine the functions.

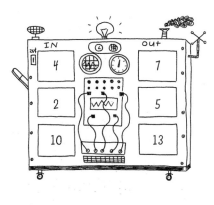

Teaching Tip

Calculator Fun

Show students how to turn their calculators into function machines. It's easy to do! Let's say you want to make the function "+2." Press "+," then "2," then "=." From now on, every time you press "=" your calculator will add 2 to the previous number. Students can program their calculators with a function and see if classmates can guess it by viewing the outputs.

ACTIVITY: **Make a Function Machine**

Use pages 48 and 49 to have students make their own Function Machines. First, have each student decide on a function and write the input and output numbers on Sheet B, based on this function. Then have them place the cover sheet over Sheet B and exchange Function Machines with a partner. The partner pulls up Sheet B until the first set of inputs and outputs appear at the cover sheet's windows. The partner continues moving up the bottom sheet, revealing new inputs and outputs until he or she correctly guesses the function. The quicker the student correctly guesses the function, the higher the score. (The number of points scored is indicated on the same line as the input/output numbers.) Students can take turns trying each other's machines and accumulating points as they practice identifying functions.

Materials

- Letter #7 (p. 52)
- transparency of Letter #7
- overhead marker
- pencil
- Practice Page #7 (pp. 54–55)
- Review Page #7 (p. 56)

ACTIVITY LESSON #7

Introducing Squid Roll-Ups

(TABLES AND FORMULAS)

Overview: Over the next three lessons, students will learn how to represent functional relationships three different ways—as tables, graphs, and formulas. It is important that students understand that all these representations are simply different ways of portraying the same relationship.

Tell the class, "We got another letter from Hibbins!" Distribute copies of Letter #7 to students and take turns reading aloud together.

Display a transparency of the letter on the overhead. Ask: "What is Hibbins's problem?" (*He doesn't know how to read the professor's table for ordering the correct number of squid.*) "How might we go about helping him?" Draw students' attention to the key below the chart that indicates X equals 2 squid. Work with students to complete the table as a class. Based on the data in the drawing, the table should look as follows:

Day Number	Squid Purchased
1	6
2	12
3	18
4	24
5	30
6	36

When the table is completed, ask the class: "What is the rule?" (*Multiply the day number by 6*) If students respond that the rule is to add 6 more each day, remind them that multiplication is repeated addition and is quicker. Ask students: "How many squid would be purchased on day number 10?" (*60*) "What about on day number 20?" (*120*) "On day number 100?" (*600*)

Most students should be able to complete the table without much difficulty, but identifying the rule might be more challenging. It is important that students get comfortable with "experimenting" with numbers to identify a pattern's rule.

It is also important for them to get comfortable with the conventions of writing formulas. In this example, the formula is:

Day Number × 6 = Number of Squid Purchased

Write this formula on the board and tell students, "When we see functional relationships like this, where two numbers are related by a function such as addition or multiplication, we can write it like this to make it easier for others to understand. We can even shorten this further by substituting the letter N to stand for Day Number and writing the formula as:

N × 6 = Squid Purchased

ACTIVITY: **Restaurant Order**

Photocopy and distribute the Restaurant Order form (p. 53) to students. Tell students: "You are a chef at your own restaurant. Fill in a name for the restaurant and tell what kind of cuisine you specialize in. Create a key for a particular ingredient you need to order and fill in the table with an order for the week. Then write a function to show how anyone reading the table could order that ingredient for additional days of food supplies." When students have completed these tables, invite them to share their charts with the class.

Literature Link

The Doorbell Rang
by Pat Hutchins
(Greenwillow, 1986)

Victoria and Sam's mother makes a plate full of cookies for the children to share, but then the doorbell starts ringing and continues to ring as more and more neighbors show up and are invited to share in the cookies. This book provides a good scenario full of data that can be organized in a chart or table form and described with formulas.

Teaching Tip

Order of Operations

If students are not familiar with order of operations, this may be a good time to introduce the concept. Explain that in a multifunction problem, multiplication and division are to be completed before addition and subtraction, unless parentheses enclose the addition or subtraction portion of the problem. For example, if the problem reads 2 + 3 × 4, we should multiply 3 × 4 first to get 12, and then add the 2 to get 14. If, however, the problems reads (2 + 3) × 4, we would add 2 + 3 first to get 5, then multiply by 4 to get 20. Parentheses and the order of operations make a big difference!

Materials

- Letter #8 (pp. 57–58)
- Practice Page #8 (pp. 59–60)
- Review Page #8 (pp. 61–62)
- pencil

Teaching Tip

Abbreviations and Symbols

In mathematics we often use abbreviations and symbols for commonly used words. In measurement, for example, we abbreviate units like inch (in.) and yard (yd.). Instead of writing the word *multiply* we use "×," and when we want to add we write "+." In formulas, we also see abbreviations, such as A for area or L for length. This helps us to communicate efficiently. Consider enlisting your students' help to put together a chart of symbols and abbreviations that are commonly used in math that students can refer to as they "translate" from one language to another.

ACTIVITY LESSON #8

Squid Roll-Ups Hit the Stores
(EXPRESSIONS AND FORMULAS)

> **Overview:** This lesson introduces students to the idea of representing functional relationships with expressions and formulas.

Announce to the class that you've received another letter from the professor. Distribute copies to students and read the letter aloud together.

Pair up students and ask them to answer the professor's questions about the first chart. When students have finished, gather the class to review their work. Ask: "What is the rule for the pattern for the 4-ounce package?" (*Weight = Number of roll-ups × 4 ounces*) Check by applying the rule to several of the numbers in the left-hand column of the chart.

Ask students: "How much would a box of 10 roll-ups weigh?" (*40 ounces*) Write "10 × 4" on the board and tell students that this expression tells how much the box weighs. Explain that an *expression* is a mathematical phrase that includes numbers and operations. For example, 7 + 6 is an expression. Notice that an expression does not include an equal sign. When you add the equal sign and show what the expression is equal to, you have an *equation*. Ask students: "What expression shows how much a package of 25 roll-ups would weigh?" (*25 × 4*) "What equation shows how much it weighs?" (*25 × 4 = 100*) A package with 25 4-ounce roll-ups would weigh 100 ounces.

Review the rule for the pattern for the 4-ounce package: **Weight = Number of roll-ups × 4**. Explain to students that there is a quicker or shorter way we can write this rule—it's called a *formula*. A formula is an equation that expresses a rule with the use of symbols. For example, for the above rule, the formula could be written as $W = N \times 4$, where W stands for weight and N stands for the number of roll-ups. You might want to introduce the term *variable* to students, explaining that a variable is a letter that stands for a number or an unknown quantity. (Note that variables will be addressed in more detail in Lesson 11.)

Call students' attention to the second chart in Professor Palindrome's letter and repeat the above steps with the second chart. In this case, the formula is $W = N \times 6$.

For additional in-class practice on this concept, you may want to begin Review Page #8 in class and have students complete the page for homework.

ACTIVITY: **Formula Finders**

Have students work together with a partner to search through their math books or the Internet to find mathematical formulas (for example, A = L × W, where A stands for area, L for length, and W for width). Students should write down the formula and two examples of applying the formula. (The formulas for area, perimeter, and volume are good, age-appropriate examples.) Then invite them to share their findings with the rest of the class.

. . . .

ACTIVITY LESSON #9

The Success of Squid Roll-Ups

(GRAPHING FUNCTIONAL RELATIONSHIPS)

Overview: Students explore how functional relationships can be represented on a graph. This lesson assumes that students have some familiarity with reading line graphs and constructing them from ordered pairs. You may want to review the following terms with students: *title*, *label*, *horizontal axis*, *vertical axis*, and *ordered pairs*.

Ask the class: "What are some ways we can represent patterns?" (*Using pictures, diagrams, charts, tables, formulas, and so on*) As an example, draw a simple function machine on the board like this one:

Ask, "What are some in and out values that this function machine would produce?" (*Answers will vary, but make sure the output number is equivalent to the input number times 3.*)

Then ask the class how they might show the in/out values as a table. Draw a grid on the board similar to the one below and ask for volunteers to fill in the missing values:

In	1	2	3	4	5
Out	3	6			

Tell the class that you are going to show them another way to represent these values. Using the values from the in/out table, write the

Materials

. . . .

- Letter #9 (p. 63)
- large piece of graph paper
- Practice Page #9 (pp. 65–66)
- Review Page #9 (p. 67)
- pencil

Literature Link

. . . .

The Grapes of Math by Greg Tang (Scholastic Press, 2001)

This book is full of clever math riddles, each shared in the form of a poem and accompanying illustration. Usually Tang challenges the reader to figure out how many of a certain item are in an illustration, and he provides a clever strategy within the context of the poem for figuring this out. Try a few of these with your class and then challenge them to see if they can write some of these strategies as expressions or formulas.

Teaching Tip

Real-Life Graphing

Ask the class what the graph at right would look like if it included ten weeks of data. Assuming the pattern was to continue, the line would continue going in the same direction—up. At this point, it would be helpful to discuss whether or not extending the line is an appropriate thing to do. In a real-life situation, would it be reasonable for a businessperson to assume that sales would continue to increase according to the pattern? Perhaps the product could catch on after a few more weeks and then skyrocket or sales might level off or even plummet. Just as business people shouldn't get caught up in the numbers that they lose sight of the underlying reality, young mathematicians need to remember the real-life connection to the mathematical situation and not just see the abstraction of numbers and graphs on a page.

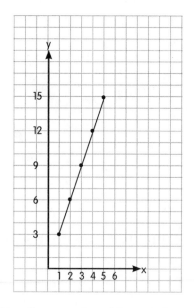

following ordered pairs on the board: (1, 3) (2, 6) (3, 9) (4, 12) (5, 15).

If the class has worked with graphing before, ask: "What do these numbers remind you of?" (*Ordered pairs used for plotting a line graph*) If necessary, review the term *ordered pair* and the concept of using *x* and *y*. If students are unfamiliar with the concept, draw a grid on the board. Explain that the values from the in/out table can be drawn on a grid. Point out the x- and y-axes and plot the x and y coordinates for each ordered pair, one at a time, until the line is complete.

Tell students that yet another letter from Professor Palindrome has arrived. Distribute copies of Letter #9 and read it aloud together. Work as a class to answer the professor's questions. Ask the class: "What is the rule for this pattern? (*Double the week number to calculate the number of roll-ups sold*) "What is the formula for this pattern?" (*Roll-ups sold = 2 × W*) "How many roll-ups would be sold in week 10?" (*20*)

Post a large piece of graph paper on the board or draw a simple grid. Tell the class that they are going to make a graph of the sales table. Say, "Sometimes displaying data on a graph is a good way to see a trend or pattern, particularly over time." Call on volunteers to title the graph and to label the horizontal and vertical axes. (Make sure that Week Number is used to label the horizontal axis. If time is a value, it is typically on the horizontal axis.)

Ask the class to name the ordered pairs that will be plotted on the graph. [(1, 2) (2, 4) (3, 6) (4, 8) (5, 10)] Call on volunteers to help plot these points on the graph. The finished product should look something like this:

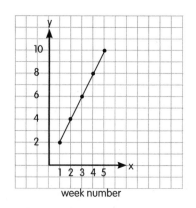

week number

Ask the class to use the graph to find the sales in week 7 *(14)* and week 9 *(18)*. Write the ordered pairs (7, 14) and (9, 18) on the board. Ask what the ordered pair for week 15 would look like. *(15, 30)*

Discuss with students how a graph, a table, and a formula are alike and how they are different. By the end of this discussion, students should understand that they are simply different ways of representing the same thing.

The extended graph will look like this:

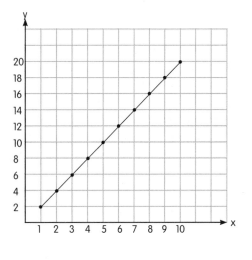

Activity: **Make-a-Graph Swap and Match**

Make a copy of Make-a-Graph (p. 64) for each student. Invite students to fill in the table with data they create. Then have them plot this data on the graph below the table. When they have finished, have students cut the paper in half. Collect the graphs and place them in one pile. Then collect the tables and place them in a separate pile. Shuffle each pile. Challenge students to match up each graph with its corresponding table. You can do this as a contest with time limits, teams, and scores or just as a practice exercise.

ACTIVITY LESSON #10

Hibbins Designs a Package for Squid Roll-Ups

(Drawings, Diagrams, and Patterns)

Overview: Students learn that drawings and diagrams can help represent patterns and other mathematical ideas.

Tell the class that another letter from Hibbins has arrived. Distribute copies of Letter #10 to students and read aloud together. Challenge students to create a package design, as per Hibbins's request, and give them time to complete their drawings or diagrams.

Teaching Tip

Using Symbols

Symbols are part of our mathematical language. Students should understand that math is indeed a language, one in which we can communicate clearly and efficiently a variety of ideas. Symbols are one of the shortcuts we use in this language. For example, we could communicate about 2 groups of 5 by writing the words *two multiplied by five equals ten*, or we could use symbols and write *2 x 5 = 10*. Have the class write some expressions and equations using words and then rewrite it using numbers and symbols. This can help students better understand and appreciate the symbolic shortcut.

Materials

- Letter #10 (p. 68)
- colored pencils/crayons
- Practice Page #10 (pp. 70–71)
- Review Page #10 (pp. 72–73)

Students' representations may range from very literal (e.g., a picture of 12 squid bodies with 10 tentacles) to something more abstract (e.g., a circle representing the squid body with the number 10 written in each circle). Students are likely to use different strategies—such as multiplication, repeated addition, or a combination of subtotals—to arrive at the total. Make sure they understand that there is no one correct way to use a drawing or diagram to represent a problem. Invite them to share and explain their designs with the class.

After reviewing students' designs, ask the class: "How could you represent this problem using numbers?" (*Answers may vary, including: 120 = 10 + 10 + 10 + 10 + 10 + 10 + 10 + 10 + 10 + 10 + 10 + 10; 120 = 12 × 10; etc.*) "How many tentacles would 8 squid have in all?" (*80*) "How many tentacles would 10 squid have in all?" (*100*) "What is the formula for calculating the number of tentacles for any number of squid?" (*Total number of tentacles = 10 × n, where n is the number of squid*)

ACTIVITY: **My Wonderful Product**

Invite students to develop a new product of their own. Give each student a copy of My Wonderful Product (p. 69). Review directions with them to make sure they understand that they should choose a product, give it a name, and draw a design for the product package. The drawing should represent a pattern, just as Hibbins's Squid Roll-Ups package did. Have students write a formula to match the drawing of the pattern.

Materials

- Letter #11 (p. 74)
- Practice Page #11 (pp. 76–77)
- Review Page #11 (p. 78)
- pencil

ACTIVITY LESSON #11

Griselda Is Tested

(*VARIABLES*)

> Overview: Students learn how variables can be used to represent a variety of mathematical ideas.

Announce to students that the latest letter from Hibbins has arrived. Distribute copies of Letter #11 to students and read aloud together.

Discuss the letter with students, saying, "In this letter, Hibbins asks us to write problems using formulas and what he calls an 'unknown.'

What do you think he means by that?" Guide students to notice in each problem there is a value that is not known. For example, in the first problem the unknown is how many toad diapers are in a box.

Explain to students that to represent an unknown quantity, we often use a *variable*. A variable is a symbol, letter, or even an empty box that stands for a quantity. Explain that in mathematics, variables can be used in many ways:

- A variable can stand for a specific unknown. For example, if $6 + x = 10$, we know that the only possible value for x is 4.

- A variable can also be used to show principles that are true for all numbers. For example, any number times 0 equals 0, or $n \times 0 = 0$.

- A variable can also be used to show quantities that vary in value. For example, in the equation $y = 2x + 7$, as x increases in value, so does y.

Have students work with a partner to solve the problems in Hibbins's letter. Then go over the answers together as a class.

For the first question, students should indicate that there are 9 diapers in each box. Answers could vary, but include $3 \times N = 27$ or $27 \div 3 = N$ or even $N + N + N = 27$. Use this opportunity to discuss the relationship between multiplication and division and the nature of fact families.

For the second question, some students will answer $M = 2 \times P$, while others may say that $P = M/2$. Again, this provides an opportunity to discuss the relationship between multiplication and division.

The third question involves more than one operation. One possible answer is $N = (22 - 2)/4$. For the fourth question, have students write their own story problem that uses the formula $24/x = 3$. Invite them to share their story problems and discuss as a group.

ACTIVITY: **How Often Do I . . . ?**

Photocopy the How Often Do I . . . ? sheet (p. 75) and distribute to students for homework. Invite students to choose an activity that they do more than once a day, such as brush their teeth or drink a glass of juice. Then have them complete the sheet using a variable to represent the number of times they do the activity in one day, one week, one month, one year, and so on. Have them write a formula that shows how often they do this activity for each time period. Ask students to share their results with the class. You might even consider making a bulletin board display of their work, using illustrations to show the various activities.

Literature Link

Spaghetti and Meatballs for All!
by Marilyn Burns
(Scholastic, 1997)

The Comfort Family decides to host a big family reunion. Mr. and Mrs. Comfort have to plan the food as well as the seating, tables, chairs, glasses, and silverware. While planning, they use lots of mathematics, including patterns, geometry, relationships, and diagrams, to make sure the big reunion all works out. As more guests arrive, they keep adjusting the plan, but in the end, the math works and the party is great!

Teaching Tip

X as a Variable

X is often used as a variable. However, when X is used as a variable in equations and expressions that involve multiplication, it's easy to confuse the multiplication sign ($\times$) with the variable (x or X). This might be a good time to teach students another common method of indicating multiplication in expressions and equations. For example, the formula Area = Length x Width can be written as A = LW (without the times sign) or as A = (L)(W). It's not too early for students to gain exposure to these ideas, which will be important as they progress in math.

Part 2: Rules and Symbols of Arithmetic

Materials

....

- Balance scale

- 1-, 5-, and 10-gram weights

- Letter #12 (pp. 79–80)

- Practice Page #12 (pp. 82–83)

- Review Page #12 (p. 84)

ACTIVITY LESSON #12

Griselda's Scale

(*BALANCING EQUATIONS*)

Overview: Students understand the concept of balancing equations with the help of balance scales.

Note: If a balance scale and weights are not available, use drawings on the board or a copy of the Balance Scale Drawings sheet (p. 81).

Show the balance scale to the class and say: "This measurement tool is called a balance scale, or balance. It is used to find weight. How does this type of scale work?" (*The object being weighed is put on one arm of the scale and weights are added to the other arm until both are level.*) Demonstrate how this works using a few small classroom items, such as erasers or glue sticks.

Place a 10-gram weight on one arm. Ask students: "How many 5-gram weights will I need to put on the other arm to balance the 10-gram weight?" (*2*) Call on a volunteer to come and put 5-gram weights, one by one, on the other arm until they balance the 10-gram weight. Point out that two 5-gram weights are the same number of grams as one 10-gram weight. Then take the two 5-gram weights off the scale and ask: "How many 1-gram weights are needed to restore balance?" (*10*) Call on another volunteer to put the 1-gram weights, one by one, on the other arm. (If you have enough balances and weights, you might want to have students work in small groups to further explore this concept. This will help reinforce their understanding of balancing weights.)

Next, introduce the concept of balancing equations by putting a 10-gram weight on one arm of the scale and, on the other arm, a 5-gram weight and two 1-gram weights. Ask the class: "Which side is heavier? (*The 10-gram weight*) How can you tell?" (*The balance is tipped toward that side.*) Use the terms *greater than* and *less than* to explain the relationship between the 10-gram weight and the 7-gram weights. On the board, write $10 > 7$ and $7 < 10$ to reinforce the concept. Then ask students: "How can we balance the scale?" (*Add 3 grams to the lighter arm*) "How might this look as an equation?" (*7 + 3 = 10*) Write the

Operations

equation on the board. Repeat with a few other examples.

Distribute copies of Letter #12 from Griselda and ask students to work with a partner to answer the questions. Review the answers together, making sure students use the terms *greater than*, *less than*, and *equal to* in their explanations. As you review each problem, rewrite the equation or inequality using numbers and the greater-than, less-than, or equal-to symbols.

ACTIVITY: **Balance Scale Drawings**

Provide each student with a copy of the Balance Scale Drawings sheet (p. 81). On the first two scales, have students use the elements in the key to draw pictures that show balanced equations. Have them write the corresponding equation under each scale. On the third scale, have students create their own elements and key and use these to show a new equation. When finished, invite students to share their drawings in class. You might want to display students' work on a bulletin board.

ACTIVITY LESSON #13

Griselda Organizes the Secret Laboratory

(COMMUTATIVE PROPERTY OF ADDITION AND MULTIPLICATION)

> Overview: Students see how the commutative properties of addition and multiplication can be expressed in algebraic terms.

Tell the class, "We have received a new letter from Griselda." Distribute copies of the letter to students and read it aloud together, pausing after Griselda's first question. Ask students: "Do you agree with Griselda or Professor Palindrome?" Write the two expressions (5 × 10 and 10 × 5) on the board. Since they are "turnaround facts" and both equal 50, students should conclude that the expressions are the same. Explain to students that this is the commutative property of multiplication.

Continue reading the letter, stopping again after the second question. Ask students: "Is 25 + 15 the same as 15 + 25?" (*Yes, the*

Teaching Tip

"Equal To" vs. "The Same As"

Emphasize to students that when they are reading algebraic equations, the equal sign (=) means "the same as." For example, the equation 4 + 4 = 2 x 4 can be read as "four plus four is the same as two times four." This will reinforce the idea of balancing equations because each side has the same quantity.

Materials

- Letter #13 (p. 85)
- Practice Page #13 (p. 86)
- Review Page #13 (p. 87)
- pencil

Literature Link

Amanda Bean's Amazing Dream by Cindy Neuschwander (Scholastic, 1999)

In this zany picture book, Amanda Bean, a girl who counts anything and everything, discovers how multiplication can help her do just that more quickly and accurately. There are lots of scenarios in which multiplication examples emerge and the idea of commutativity can be applied while reinforcing to students why it is indeed important to commit multiplication facts to memory.

Materials

- plain paper
- colored pencils/crayons
- Letter #14 (pp. 88–89)
- Practice Page #14 (p. 90)
- Review Page #14 (p. 91)

commutative property of addition says it is the same.) Explain that the commutative property works for both multiplication and addition. We can use variables to write a formula that shows it is true. On the board, write $a + b = b + a$, telling students that this equation shows the commutative property of addition. Encourage students to plug in any numbers for a and b to see that this is true.

Ask the class: "If we were to write a formula using variables for the commutative property of multiplication, how would that look?" ($a \times b = b \times a$) Call on student volunteers to plug in any numbers for a and b to see that this formula is also always true.

Challenge students to write three examples of commutativity for addition and three for multiplication. Encourage students to see if they can use variables in at least one example. Have them share their equations and discuss them in class.

ACTIVITY: **Extending Commutativity**

Have students see if they can extend the concept of commutativity to more than two variables. Ask the class to write three examples for the commutative property of addition using three, four, and five variables. Then have them do the same for multiplication.

ACTIVITY LESSON #14

Griselda and the FOOL
(OTHER PROPERTIES OF ADDITION AND MULTIPLICATION)

> **Overview:** Students look at other properties of addition and multiplication and how they can be described algebraically.

Announce to the class: "We have another letter from Griselda." Distribute copies of Letter #14 to students and read it aloud together.

Look at the first question and discuss which arrangement of addends is most efficient and why. (*17 + 13 + 12 = 42. It is easier to add 17 and 13 first for a subtotal of 30. Then add 12 for a sum of 42.*)

Explain to students that the associative property of addition allows us to reorder the addends and still get the same answer. Write on the board the following equation: $(a + b) + c = a + (b + c)$. If necessary, invite students to plug in numbers for each variable to prove that this property is correct. The same thing applies for multiplication. The associative property of multiplication allows us to reorder the factors and still get the same answer. Write this equation on the board: $(a \times b) \times c = a \times (b \times c)$. The associative property of multiplication is particularly useful to students when they are still mastering multiplication. Arranging the factors in a certain order can make a problem easier to solve. Discuss these ideas as you work on questions one and two.

For the second question, invite students to share their arrangements and explain why they chose them. *(The factors can be arranged as $4 \times 8 \times 10$. It is relatively easy to multiply 32×10 to get the product of 320.)*

As students master basic multiplication facts, they learn that 1 times a number equals that number (the identity property of multiplication) and that 0 times a number equals 0 (the zero property of multiplication). Touch back on these ideas as you discuss questions three and four. *($1 \times 365 = 365$; $90 \times 0 = 0$)*

On the other hand, any number added to 0 will equal that number (the identity property of addition). Discuss this property as you work together on question five. *($16 + 0 = 16$)*

As you work through these problems, write the properties, their names, and examples with both variables and numbers plugged in. Explain to students, "Properties like these are useful in solving problems, particularly in balancing and solving equations. We can rely on these rules to help simplify problems that can get very complex."

ACTIVITY: **Algebra Concentration**

Create an algebra concentration game to help students review the algebra terms they've learned (such as *formula*, *expression*, and *pattern*) as well as the various properties of addition and multiplication. Partner up students and give each pair a set of index cards. Have students divide the cards into two piles. On the cards in one pile, have them write a property of addition or multiplication or a term they have learned during this unit. On the other pile of cards, have them write some examples that correspond to each property or term. Shuffle the newly made deck of cards and deal them facedown in rows. Players take turns flipping over a card and then turning over another card to find a match. If the cards match, the player keeps both cards. Play continues until all the cards are gone.

Professor Percy Palindrome

World-Famous Scientist, Inventor Extraordinaire (and Lawns Mowed)

Greetings, Young Scientists and Mathematicians!

Allow me to introduce myself. I am Professor Percy Palindrome, possibly the world's greatest inventor. I conduct my experiments in my secret laboratory with Hibbins, my loyal assistant.

I've been trying to communicate with an alien civilization living on a planet that orbits the star Sirius. I decided to send them my formula for toenail cleaner, one of my most impressive inventions. To make sure they received the message, I transmitted the formula by radio, repeating it several times. This is what the message looked like:

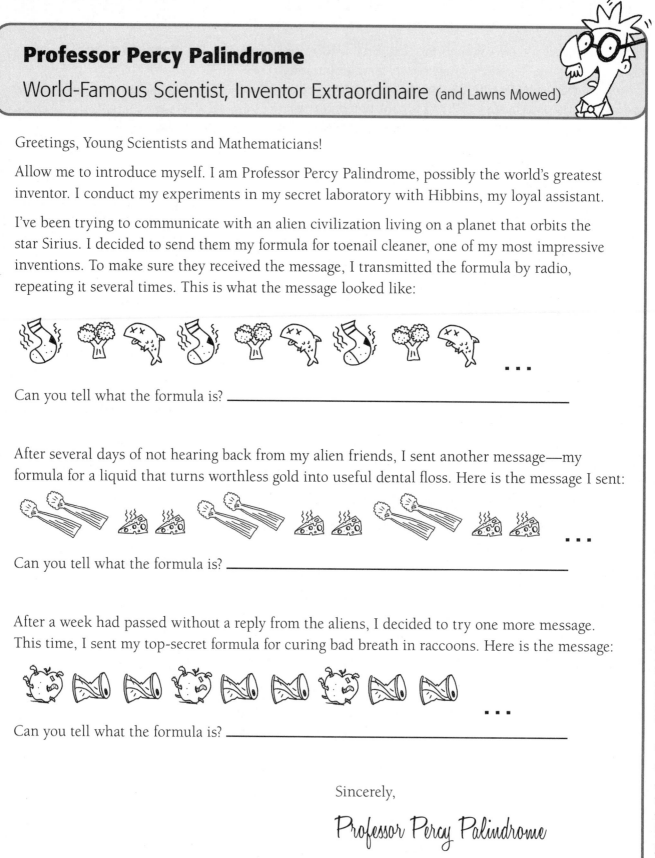

Can you tell what the formula is? _____

After several days of not hearing back from my alien friends, I sent another message—my formula for a liquid that turns worthless gold into useful dental floss. Here is the message I sent:

Can you tell what the formula is? _____

After a week had passed without a reply from the aliens, I decided to try one more message. This time, I sent my top-secret formula for curing bad breath in raccoons. Here is the message:

Can you tell what the formula is? _____

Sincerely,

Professor Percy Palindrome

Reteaching Math: Algebra Readiness © 2008 by Bob Krech, Scholastic Teaching Resources

Name: _____ Date: _____

Reteaching Math: Algebra Readiness © 2008 by Bob Krech, Scholastic Teaching Resources

WORD PROBLEM

Terri was decorating her notebook with stickers. She arranged them this way: baseball, football, soccer ball, baseball, football, soccer ball. How many elements are in her pattern? What are the elements? What is the core of her pattern?

BASICS BOX

Element – A single symbol in a pattern. In the pattern ABCABCABC, the letters A, B, and C are the elements.

Core – The smallest combination of elements that repeats in a pattern. In the pattern ABCABCABC, "ABC" is the core.

Recurring pattern – A pattern that repeats

In Terri's sticker pattern, the three elements are baseball, football, and soccer ball. The core is baseball, football, soccer ball. If we were to use letters to describe this pattern it would look like this: ABCABC.

PRACTICE

Using pictures or symbols, create your own recurring pattern in the boxes below. When you're finished, switch papers with a classmate and solve each other's patterns.

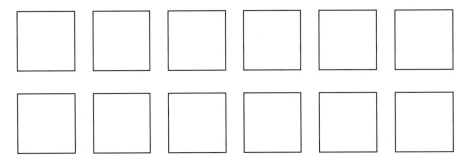

1. How many elements are in your pattern?

_____

What are they?

_____

2. What is the core of your pattern?

_____

3. Describe your core using letters.

_____

JOURNAL

Are there any recurring patterns in your house? (Hint: Look at the floor and walls.) Describe the patterns you find.

Name: _____ Date: _____

Recurring Patterns

1. Fill in the boxes with the next three symbols in the pattern.
   Explain how you figured this out.

2. Fill in the boxes with the next four symbols in the pattern.

3. Create the pattern from number 2, using letters instead of symbols.

   _____, _____, _____, _____, _____, _____, _____, _____, . . .

4. What would the 20th element of this pattern be? _____

5. Using symbols of your choice, create an ABBA pattern below:

   _____, _____, _____, _____, _____, _____, _____, _____

6. What would the 13th element of this pattern be? _____

7. Fill in the blanks for these two patterns:

   A, B, A, C, A, B, A, C, A, B, _____, _____, _____

   1, 2, 1, 3, 1, 2, 1, 3, 1, 2, 1, _____, _____, _____

8. Are these two patterns the same or different? Explain. _____

   _____

Reteaching Math: Algebra Readiness © 2008 by Bob Krech, Scholastic Teaching Resources

From the Desk of Hibbins

Loyal Assistant to Professor Percy Palindrome

My Dear Young Scientists and Mathematicians:

I am Hibbins, loyal assistant to Professor Percy Palindrome. I do my best to keep him on track. I also feed our laboratory animals—they're really more like pets. One of my favorites is the "flaboon," a creature the professor created by crossing a fly with a baboon. The flaboon has a sensitive stomach and must be fed according to a special schedule. The feeding schedule looks like this:

Day 1	Day 2	Day 3	Day 4	Day 5	Day 6
Avocado	**B**eet	**C**antaloupe	**A**vocado	**B**eet	**C**antaloupe

The feeding schedule is a recurring pattern. Can you find the core? _____
(Use the first letter of each food if you like.)

What will the flaboon eat on the 8th day? _____

What will the flaboon eat on the 12th day? _____

I also have a regular schedule of chores to attend to in the laboratory. My chore schedule is on the chart at right:

My chore schedule is also a recurring pattern. Can you find the core? (Use the first letter of each chore if you like.)

Day 1	**P**olish the plutonium prune pitter
Day 2	**B**ack up the bagel bisector
Day 3	**A**lign the atomic accordion
Day 4	**A**lign the atomic accordion
Day 5	**P**olish the plutonium prune pitter
Day 6	**B**ack up the bagel bisector
Day 7	**A**lign the atomic accordion
Day 8	**A**lign the atomic accordion

_____

What chore do you think I'll be doing on day 11? _____

What chore do you think I'll be doing on day 16? _____

Sincerely,

Hibbins

Name: _____ Date: _____

Jake is an eating champion. He eats a doughnut, bagel, waffle, and another bagel every hour in that order. It is 8:00 A.M. and he is just beginning to eat. What time will it be when Jake eats his sixth bagel?

BASICS BOX

Element – A single symbol in a pattern. In the pattern ABCABC, the letters A, B, and C are the elements.

Core – The smallest combination of elements that repeats in a pattern. To predict how a pattern will continue, repeat the core as often as needed.

The elements in Jake's pattern are doughnut, bagel, and waffle. The core is doughnut, bagel, waffle, bagel, or DBWB. We can extend the pattern and see when the sixth bagel will be eaten:

8:00 A.M. DBWB

9:00 A.M. DBWB

10:00 A.M. DBWB

We can see that Jake eats his sixth bagel at 10:00 A.M.

PRACTICE

Professor Palindrome's latest invention is a combination of a cotton plant and sugar cane. The result: a cotton candy plant. He has been observing how his new plants start out as seeds, become seedlings, and then plants with taller stalks. When they are fully mature, the cotton candy flowers bloom. Yum! Before they die, the plants make seeds for the next generation of plants.

1. Professor Palindrome is a bit absent-minded and doesn't always remember to record his observations. Look at the pattern and fill in the missing entries.

2. What would the 25th observation look like? _____

JOURNAL

Explain how you filled in Professor Palindrome's missing observations and determined what the 25th observation would look like. How do you know you are right?

Reteaching Math: Algebra Readiness © 2008 by Bob Krech, Scholastic Teaching Resources

Name: _____ Date: _____

Extending and Predicting Patterns

1. Fill in the blanks to create a repeating pattern with a core of ABCD.

    _____, _____, _____, _____, _____, _____, _____, _____, _____

    What would be the 12th element of this pattern? _____

2. 1, 2, 2, 1, 1, 2, 2, 1, 1, 2, 2, 1, . . .

    What is the core of this pattern? _____

    What would be the 14th element of this pattern? _____

3. ¢, *, !, ¢, *, !, ¢, . . .

    What would be the 11th element of this pattern? _____

    What would be the 18th element of this pattern? _____

    How did you figure out the 18th element of this pattern? _____

4. Fill in the blanks to create a repeating pattern with a core of ABAC.

    _____, _____, _____, _____, _____, _____, _____, _____, _____, . . .

    What would be the 21st element of this pattern? _____

5.  ☺ ♪ ♩ ☺ ☺ ♪ ♩ ☺ ☺ ♪ ♩ ☺ ...

    What would be the 13th element of this pattern? _____

    What would be the 22nd element of this pattern? _____

    How did you figure out the 22nd element of this pattern? _____

6. △ ▢ △ ◯ △ ▢ △ ◯ △ ▢ ...

    What is the core of this pattern? _____

7. △ △ ◯ ◯ △ △ ◯ ◯ ...

    Create the same pattern using letters:

    _____, _____, _____, _____, _____, _____, _____, _____, _____, . . .

Professor Percy Palindrome

World-Famous Scientist, Inventor Extraordinaire (and Lawns Mowed)

Greetings, Young Scientists and Mathematicians!

Much to my delight, I have received a reply from the aliens on the planet near the star Sirius! Hibbins mumbled something about this defying the laws of physics, but I just ignored him. The message is a bit strange, and some of it didn't come in clearly, but I have a feeling you can help me figure it out. This is what the message looked like:

	Us	Alone	Leave	Us
Alone	Leave	Us	Alone	Leave
Us		Leave		Alone
	Us	Alone	Leave	
	Leave			

What is the aliens' message? _____

Can you figure out the missing parts of the message? Write them in the blank spaces in the message grid.

What would the next line of the message look like?

Sincerely,

Professor Percy Palindrome

Reteaching Math: Algebra Readiness © 2008 by Bob Krech, Scholastic Teaching Resources

Name: _____ Date: _____

Jasmine practices her flute only on Thursdays. If today is Monday, the 5th of April, what will be the last practice date for Jasmine this month?

BASICS BOX

Patterns are not always arranged in a straight line. Many patterns—such as calendars, number charts, and some timetables—are arranged in grids.
We can solve Jasmine's problem by drawing a calendar. The pattern of her practice days and the pattern of the dates on the calendar will help us determine the answer.

Su	M	Tu	W	Th	F	Sa
				1	2	3
4	5	6	7	8	9	10
11	12	13	14	15	16	17
18	19	20	21	22	23	24
25	26	27	28	29	30	

We can see by the calendar above that her last practice date will be Thursday, April 29th.

PRACTICE

Professor Palindrome was shocked to learn that the aliens wanted him to leave them alone. To feel better, he decided to tile the laboratory walls.

1. The professor particularly likes the ABCABC recurring pattern and has decided to use these tiles. Complete the design in the drawing below.

2. If we added two rows to the bottom of the design, what symbol would appear in the lower left corner?

_____

JOURNAL

Explain how you completed the design. How did you determine the symbol that would appear in the lower left corner if two rows were added to the design? Create your own grid design using a recurring pattern.

Reteaching Math: Algebra Readiness © 2008 by Bob Krech, Scholastic Teaching Resources

37

Name: _____   Date: _____

Positioning Patterns on Grids

1. Fill in the missing elements in this grid.

A	B	B	A	A
B	B	A	A	B
B	A		B	B
	A		B	
	B	B		

If a sixth row were added to the grid, what would it look like?

2. Fill in the missing elements in this grid.

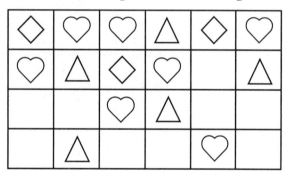

If a sixth row were added to the grid, what would it look like?

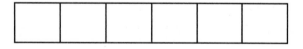

3. Fill in the grid with a recurring pattern with a core of ABAC.

If the pattern continued, what would the 30th element be? _____

4. Pattern #1

A	B	B	A	A
B	B	A	A	B
B	A	A	B	B
A	A	B	B	A

Pattern #2

A	B	B	A
A	B	B	A
A	B	B	A
A	B	B	A
A	B	B	A

How are these patterns alike? _____

How are they different? _____

Review:

5. A, B, A, C, A, B, A, C, A, . . .

What is the 25th element of this pattern? _____

6. A, B, B, C, A, B, B, C, A, B, B, . . .

What is the core of this pattern? _____

Reteaching Math: Algebra Readiness © 2008 by Bob Krech, Scholastic Teaching Resources

Professor Percy Palindrome

World-Famous Scientist, Inventor Extraordinaire (and Lawns Mowed)

Greetings, Young Scientists and Mathematicians!

Although my first cotton candy plant experiment has failed, I intend to learn from my mistakes. I experimented with two varieties of cotton plants to develop the world's first cotton candy plant. One variety was from the nation of Bulgaria, while the other was from Senegal. The two cotton candy plants grew differently. Although the Bulgarian plant grew faster for the first few days, the Senegalese plant eventually caught up and passed it. Here are the growth charts for both varieties:

Growth Chart – Bulgarian Cotton Candy Plant						
Height (in inches)	1"	4"	7"	10"	13"	16"
Day	1	2	3	4	5	6

Can you determine how tall the plant will be on day 7? _____

Growth Chart – Senegalese Cotton Candy Plant						
Height (in inches)	1"	2"	4"	8"	16"	32"
Day	1	2	3	4	5	6

Can you determine how tall the plant will be on day 7? _____

Sincerely,

Professor Percy Palindrome

Name: _____ Date: _____

Malik was counting the blocks in the tower he built. There was 1 on the top, 3 in the next level, 5 in the next level, 7 in the next level, and 9 in the next level. There was one more level under that. How many blocks were in the bottom level?

BASICS BOX

Growing pattern or sequence –
A pattern that grows, where elements have a relationship to each other. For example, in the pattern 2, 4, 6, 8, 10 . . . each number increases by 2.

Rule – The description of how a pattern changes from one element to the next. Sometimes the rule is based on a single arithmetic operation (addition, subtraction, etc.), but sometimes it can be based on more than one operation.

A good way to discover a pattern is to look at the relationship between elements in the pattern. For example, in Malik's tower you might look at the first two elements and notice that 3 is 2 more than 1. Perhaps the rule is to add 2 each time. Try out that idea on the next element and it still works: 3 + 2 = 5. Always try the rule on at least three or four elements to make sure it holds. If we add 2 more to the 9, we find that Malik had 11 blocks on the bottom of his tower.

But be careful! In a pattern like 1, 3, 9, 27, 81, adding 2 works for the first element (1 + 2 = 3), but after that the rule no longer works. Try something else. Look at the relationship between 3 and 9. It could be adding 6 or it could be multiplying by 3. Try those rules out on the next two numbers and you find that the rule is multiply by 3.

PRACTICE

Find the rule that explains how the pattern continues.

	Pattern	Rule
1.	2, 4, 6, 8, 10, . . .	_____
2.	1, 2, 4, 8, 16, . . .	_____
3.	1, 3, 7, 15, 31, . . .	_____
4.	1, 4, 9, 16, 25, . . .	_____
5.	32, 28, 24, 20, 16, . . .	_____
6.	2, 3, 5, 9, 17, 33, . . .	_____
7.	40, 39, 37, 34, 30, . . .	_____

JOURNAL

How is the pattern 1, 2, 3, 1, 2, 3, 1, 2, 3, . . . different from 2, 4, 6, 8, 10, 12, . . . ? Use the words *element*, *pattern*, *core*, *recurring pattern*, and *growing pattern* in your explanation.

Reteaching Math: Algebra Readiness © 2008 by Bob Krech, Scholastic Teaching Resources

Name: _____   Date: _____

Growing Patterns and Rules

Fill in the missing elements of each pattern.

1. 85, 75, 65, 55, 45, _____, _____, _____

2. 12, 24, 36, _____, 60, _____, _____

3. ½, 1, 1½, _____, 2½, 3, _____, 4, _____

4. _____, 14, 21, 28, _____, _____, 49

5. 64, _____, 16, 8, _____, _____, 1

6. 3, 5, _____, 12, _____, 23, 30

7. 6, 12, _____, 24, _____, _____, 42

8. 22, 33, 44, 55, _____, _____, _____

What is this pattern's rule? Explain your thinking. _____

9. 16, 8, 4, _____, 1, _____, _____, . . .

What is this pattern's rule? Explain your thinking. _____

10. 1, 3, 1, 3, 6, 1, 3, 1, 3, 6, 1, 3, _____, _____, _____, . . .

What kind of pattern is this? _____

11. Does a growing pattern have a core? Explain your answer. _____

_____

Review:

12. Complete the grid.

5	3	4	2	5	3	
2	5	3		2		3
4	2			4	2	
		2	5			

13. A, B, A, D, A, B, A, D . . .
What is the 17th element of this pattern?

_____

14. What is the 80th element of this pattern?

_____

From the Desk of Hibbins

Loyal Assistant to Professor Percy Palindrome

My Dear Young Scientists and Mathematicians:

I have been worried about Professor Palindrome. He seems upset by his recent failures in the laboratory, so I thought I would cheer him up with a new pet. I've been working in the lab myself and have created the "flop," which is a combination of a flamingo and an opossum. My first flop weighed 2 grams at birth, and then grew a bit each day. This chart shows its growth:

First Flop's Growth				
Day	Monday	Tuesday	Wednesday	Thursday
Weight (in grams)	2	5	8	11

How much do you think the flop will weigh on Friday? _____

How about on Saturday? _____

The flop was lonely, so I decided to breed another flop to keep it company. This chart shows the growth of my second flop:

Second Flop's Growth				
Day	Monday	Tuesday	Wednesday	Thursday
Weight (in grams)	1	4	7	10

How much do you think this flop will weigh on Friday? _____

How about on Saturday? _____

Which flop grew faster? Explain your answer. _____

Sincerely,

Hibbins

Reteaching Math: Algebra Readiness © 2008 by Bob Krech, Scholastic Teaching Resources

Name: _____ Date: _____

One Hundred Chart

1	2	3	4	5	6	7	8	9	10
11	12	13	14	15	16	17	18	19	20
21	22	23	24	25	26	27	28	29	30
31	32	33	34	35	36	37	38	39	40
41	42	43	44	45	46	47	48	49	50
51	52	53	54	55	56	57	58	59	60
61	62	63	64	65	66	67	68	69	70
71	72	73	74	75	76	77	78	79	80
81	82	83	84	85	86	87	88	89	90
91	92	93	94	95	96	97	98	99	100

You will see interesting patterns by "experimenting" with odd and even start and jump numbers.

1. Pick an even start number and an odd jump number.

   What are the first six elements of the pattern you made? _____

2. Pick an even start number and an even jump number.

   What are the first six elements of the pattern you made? _____

3. Pick an odd start number and an odd jump number.

   What are the first six elements of the pattern you made? _____

4. Pick an odd start number and an even jump number.

   What are the first six elements of the pattern you made? _____

5. What conclusions can you and your partner make about how odd and even numbers act when added together in different combinations?

   _____

Reteaching Math: Algebra Readiness © 2008 by Bob Krech, Scholastic Teaching Resources

Name: _____ Date: _____

Reteaching Math: Algebra Readiness © 2008 by Bob Krech, Scholastic Teaching Resources

WORD PROBLEM

Joel was in a race across a number line with Pina. Pina finished on the number 12. Joel finished on the number 10. They each moved one space ten times. What number did Pina start on? How about Joel?

3 7 11

BASICS BOX

Start number – The first number of a pattern. In the pattern 4, 6, 8, 10, . . . , 4 is the start number.

Jump number – The amount a pattern changes from element to element. In the pattern 4, 6, 8, 10 . . . , the rule is to add 2 to get the next element. 2 is the jump number.

Joel and Pina both had the same jump number (+1), but their start numbers were different. If Pina moved 10 times she must have started on 2. Joel must have started on 0.

JOURNAL

Create a pattern that has all even or all odd numbers. Then create another pattern that alternates odd and even numbers. What do you notice about the start and jump numbers in the two patterns?

PRACTICE

In a flash of brilliance, Professor Palindrome invented the solar-powered pogo stick! The professor set up a pogo-stick testing area behind the lab. Look at the results of his test jumps and answer the questions.

1. 3   7   11   _____   19   _____

    What is the start number for this pattern? _____

    What is the jump number for this pattern? _____

    What do you notice about even jump numbers with an odd start number? _____

2. 1   6   11   _____   21   _____

    What is the start number for this pattern? _____

    What is the jump number for this pattern? _____

    What do you notice about odd jump numbers with an odd start number? _____

3. 2   7   12   17   _____   27

    What is the start number for this pattern? _____

    What is the jump number for this pattern? _____

    What do you notice about odd jump numbers with an even start number? _____

4. 2   12   _____   32   _____   _____

    What is the start number for this pattern? _____

    What is the jump number for this pattern? _____

    What do you notice about even jump numbers with even start numbers? _____

Name: _____   Date: _____

Start and Jump Numbers

1. 5, 11, 17, 23, 29, 35

   What is the start number? _____   What is the jump number? _____

2. 10, 14, 18, 22, 16, 30

   What is the start number? _____   What is the jump number? _____

3. 4, 13, 22, 31, 40, 49

   What is the start number? _____   What is the jump number? _____

4. 18, 21, 24, 27, 30, 33

   What is the start number? _____   What is the jump number? _____

5. Create a pattern with a start number of 7 and a jump number of 5.

   _____, _____, _____, _____, _____, _____, _____, _____, _____, _____

6. Create a pattern with a start number of 3 and a jump number of 10.

   _____, _____, _____, _____, _____, _____, _____, _____, _____, _____

7. Create a pattern with an even start number and an odd jump number.

   _____, _____, _____, _____, _____, _____, _____, _____, _____, _____

8. A 7 B 7 7 A 7 B 7 7 A 7 B 7 7 . . .

   a. What is the core of this pattern? _____

   b. What will the 25th element be? _____

   c. What kind of pattern is it? _____

Review:

9. 4, 8, 12, 16, 20 . . .

   What is the rule? _____

10. 2, $3\frac{1}{2}$, 5, $6\frac{1}{2}$, 8 . . .

    What is the rule? _____

11. 1, 3, 9, 27, 81 . . .

    What is the rule? _____

12. 20, $17\frac{1}{2}$, 15, $12\frac{1}{2}$, 10 . . .

    What is the rule? _____

Reteaching Math: Algebra Readiness © 2008 by Bob Krech, Scholastic Teaching Resources

From the Desk of Hibbins

Loyal Assistant to Professor Percy Palindrome

My Dear Young Scientists and Mathematicians:

I'm sorry to inform you that Professor Palindrome has really gone too far this time! He is planning a dinner for some distinguished scientists he used to work with at Sawbone University. Unfortunately, he wants to serve them omelets made from lizard eggs and artificial toast made from tree bark. He predicts that each guest will eat 1 omelet and that we will need 3 eggs for each omelet. He also predicts that each guest will eat 2 pieces of toast. Neither the professor nor I will be eating. (We know better.) Please help me plan the dinner:

1. If there are 3 guests:

    a. How many omelets will I make? _____

    b. How many eggs will I need? _____

    c. How many pieces of toast will I make? _____

2. If there are 5 guests:

    a. How many omelets will I make? _____

    b. How many eggs will I need? _____

    c. How many pieces of toast will I make? _____

Sincerely,

Hibbins

Reteaching Math: Algebra Readiness © 2008 by Bob Krech, Scholastic Teaching Resources

Name: _____   Date: _____

Function Machines

Directions:

Decide on a function for each machine (for example, −2). Then fill in the IN and OUT numbers on each machine, based on its function. Remember, the function should apply to all the numbers in the machine. When you are finished, trade papers with a partner to see if he or she can determine the function of each machine.

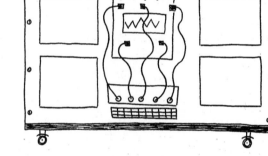

IN	OUT
10	8
7	5
3	1

Function ____−2____

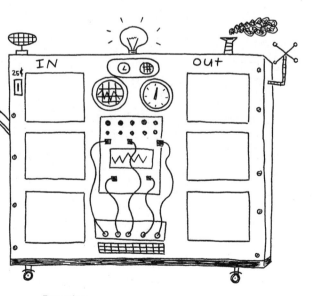

Function _____

Function _____

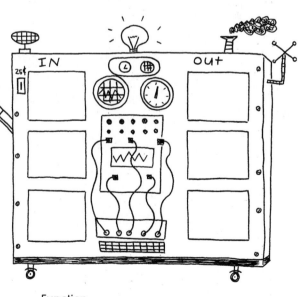

Function _____

Function _____

Name: _____   Date: _____

Function Machine (Cover)

Input   **Output**

cut out   cut out

Directions:

1.   Think of a function; for example, +7.

2.   On Sheet B, fill in the input numbers on
     the left side of the chart. Then fill in the
     output numbers that would result by
     adding 7 to the input numbers. For example,
     if the input number on the first row is 3,
     the output number would be 10 (3 + 7 = 10).
     Fill in all nine rows.

3.   Place this cover over Sheet B.

4.   Have your partner pull up the tab one row
     at a time so that the input and output numbers
     are revealed in the boxes.

5.   Challenge your partner to guess the function.
     Your partner will score points according to
     how quickly he or she guesses the function.

Reteaching Math: Algebra Readiness © 2008 by Bob Krech, Scholastic Teaching Resources

Function Machine (Sheet B)

	INPUT	[TAB – pull here]	OUTPUT	POINTS
1.				10
2.				9
3.				8
4.				7
5.				6
6.				5
7.				4
8.				3
9.				2

Reteaching Math: Algebra Readiness © 2008 by Bob Krech, Scholastic Teaching Resources

Name: _____   Date: _____

Jung is making pizzas for her sleepover. She needs 25 olives for each pizza. She has invited 12 friends. Jung, her sister, and her mom will eat also. If she makes 1 pizza for every 5 people, how many olives will she need?

BASICS BOX

Function – A relation where elements of one set are associated with one or more elements of another set.

In Jung's problem, the number of olives she needs is dependent on the number of pizzas she needs. Since there are 15 people eating (12 friends + 3 family members), and Jung plans to make 1 pizza for every 5 people, she will need 3 pizzas. We know that every pizza gets 25 olives, so 25 x 3 = 75 olives. The number of olives is a function of the number of pizzas.

PRACTICE

Professor Palindrome has been slaving away in his laboratory to develop a spray-on repellent to keep dragons away. Hibbins wondered out loud why anyone would need such a product. The professor replies, "We haven't seen a dragon around here since I started. Proof that it works!" His lab notebook includes a record of how many cans he produced each day.

Fill in the missing data from the chart and answer the questions.

Day Number	1	2	3	4	5	6	7
Cans Made	2	4	6	8	10	12	

1. How many cans would Professor Palindrome make on Day 10? _____

2. What is the rule for this pattern? _____

3. Is this a functional relationship? Why or why not?

    _____

Describe a functional relationship you have found in your kitchen at home. Hint: Check cookbooks and cooking instructions on food boxes.

Name: _____   Date: _____

Functions and Functional Relationships

Fill in the function for each set of numbers. The function may include more than one operation.

	INPUT	Function	OUTPUT
1.	15	→ ☐ →	26
	7	→ ☐ →	18
	4	→ ☐ →	15
2.	11	→ ☐ →	23
	9	→ ☐ →	19
	20	→ ☐ →	41
3.	42	→ ☐ →	21
	16	→ ☐ →	8
	27	→ ☐ →	13 ½
4.	17	→ ☐ →	33
	9	→ ☐ →	17
	20	→ ☐ →	39

Can you think of more than one function for this machine?

5.	2	→ ☐ →	4
	2	→ ☐ →	4

Review:

6. 7, 10, 13, 16, 19

What is the start number? _____ What is the jump number? _____

7. If a pattern has an even start number and an odd jump number, will the 5th element of the pattern be odd or even? _____

From the Desk of Hibbins

Loyal Assistant to Professor Percy Palindrome

My Dear Young Scientists
and Mathematicians:

Professor Palindrome sometimes makes
strange requests. Now he has asked that
I start purchasing squid for his next
invention. He asked me to purchase the
squid according to a schedule that he
says follows a pattern. But he has drawn
symbols instead of using numbers. See the
chart at right.

Squid Purchasing Schedule	
Day Number	Squid Purchased
1	×××
2	××××××
3	×××××××××
4	××××××××××××
5	×××××××××××××××
6	××××××××××××××××××

Key: × = 2 squid

My young friends, I would be most
grateful if you could help me by filling
in this squid order sheet with numbers,
not symbols.

Squid Purchasing Schedule	
Day Number	Squid Purchased
1	
2	
3	
4	
5	
6	

Professor Palindrome says that if I'm
clever and figure out the rule for his
ordering pattern, I would know how many
squid to order just by using the rule and
the day number. Please explain this to me
in the space below:

_____

_____

Sincerely,

Hibbins

Reteaching Math: Algebra Readiness © 2008 by Bob Krech, Scholastic Teaching Resources

Name: _____ Date: _____

Restaurant Order

Head Chef (you!) _____

Name of Restaurant _____

Type of Cuisine _____

Directions: Fill in the ordering key for an ingredient you need. Then fill in the order for the week. Show a pattern and a functional relationship between the days and the number of ingredients ordered. What is the rule? _____

Ordering Key	
Ingredient	**Number of Items to Order**
Example: eggs	12
_____	

Order of the Week		How Many of the Ingredient?
Sunday	Day 1	
Monday	Day 2	
Tuesday	Day 3	
Wednesday	Day 4	
Thursday	Day 5	
Friday	Day 6	
Saturday	Day 7	

Reteaching Math: Algebra Readiness © 2008 by Bob Krech, Scholastic Teaching Resources

Name: _____ Date: _____

Due to an emergency, Marlene, chef at the Ptomaine Café, had to leave the restaurant for the night. She assigned Seymore, the dishwasher, to be chef for the night. "I don't know how many meatballs to make," wailed Seymore. "It's simple," replied Marlene. "I'll make you a chart."

Orders	1	2	3	4
Meatballs	4	8	12	16

Seymore's crying subsided a bit, but then he thought, "What if more than 4 people order Meatball Surprise?" Help Seymore by finding the rule that tells how many meatballs to make for each order. Then write the rule as a formula.

BASICS BOX

Table – A tool for showing data in an organized way. Tables are usually arranged in rows and columns. Tables make it easier to see patterns.

Rule – The description of the operation (addition, subtraction, multiplication, division, or a combination of these) that is used on an input to calculate an output. For example, if the rule is to add 10 and the input number is 4, the output would be 14 (4 + 10).

Formula – An equation that states a rule or fact. A formula is more formal than a rule and includes an equal sign. For example, Out = In + 10 is a formula.

The rule for how many meatballs Seymore should make is the number of orders multiplied by 4. As a formula, this would be written Meatballs = Orders x 4.

When trying to figure out the rule for a growing pattern, look at the way the numbers increase or decrease. Remember, the rule can be based on one or more of the arithmetic operations.

PRACTICE

Noticing the popularity of fruit roll-ups, Professor Palindrome thought that Squid Roll-Ups would be a sure-fire winner. "After all," he reasoned, "squid has a nice, chewy texture, and everyone loves that yummy squid flavor." After perfecting the formula, he ordered Hibbins to start making packs of the roll-ups in the lab. The chart shows how many packs Hibbins made each day.

Day Number	Packs Made
1	××××
2	×××××
3	×××××××
4	×××××××××
5	×××××××××××

Key: × = 2 packs of Squid Roll-Ups

Reteaching Math: Algebra Readiness © 2008 by Bob Krech, Scholastic Teaching Resources

(continued)

Name: _____ Date: _____

1. On the table at right, write the number of packs made each day. What is the rule for the pattern in the table?

   _____

Day Number	Packs Made
1	
2	
3	
4	
5	

2. If the pattern continues, how many packs will Hibbins make on Day 10?

   _____

3. If the pattern continues, how many packs will Hibbins make on Day 20? _____

4. If you knew the day number, how could you determine the number of packs Hibbins made that day? _____

Suppose Professor Palindrome ordered Hibbins to make Squid Roll-Ups according to the pattern at right:

5. What is the rule for this pattern?

   _____

6. If the pattern continues, how many packs will Hibbins make on Day 10?

   _____

7. If the pattern continues, how many packs will Hibbins make on Day 20?

   _____

Day Number	Packs Made
1	××××××
2	××××××××××
3	××××××××××××××
4	××××××××××××××××××
5	××××××××××××××××××××××
6	×××××××××××××××× ××××××××××

Key: × = 2 packs

8. If you knew the day number, how could you determine the number of packs Hibbins made that day? _____

_____

JOURNAL

When you think you have figured out the rule for a pattern, how do you check to make sure it is correct?

Name: _____   Date: _____

Tables and Formulas

Find the rule. Remember, more than one operation may be used.

1.

In	Out
1	5
2	10
3	15
4	20
5	25

a. What is the rule
for this pattern? _____

b. What would the output be
if the input were 20? _____

2.

In	Out
1	3
2	5
3	7
4	9
5	11

a. What is the rule
for this pattern? _____

b. What would the output be
if the input were 10? _____

3.

In	Out
1	6
2	9
3	12
4	15
5	18

a. What is the rule
for this pattern? _____

b. What would the output be
if the input were 25? _____

4.

In	Out
1	4
2	9
3	14
4	19
5	24

a. What is the rule
for this pattern? _____

b. What would the output be
if the input were 25? _____

c. Write the rule as a formula.

_____

Professor Percy Palindrome

World-Famous Scientist, Inventor Extraordinaire (and Lawns Mowed)

Greetings, Young Scientists and Mathematicians!

Hibbins informed me that he has written to you about Squid Roll-Ups! When we start selling the roll-ups, we will have to put them in packages and pay a shipping company to deliver them to the billions of people who can't wait to eat them. The shipping company charges according to the weight of the package. The higher the weight, the higher the charge.

I'm thinking of introducing the 4-ounce Squid Roll-Ups first. It's perfect for a snack! Here's a chart showing how heavy the packages would be, depending on the number of roll-ups in each box.

Number of Roll-Ups	Weight (in ounces)	Shipping Cost
1	4	$2
2	8	$4
3	12	$6
4	16	$8
5	20	$10

The numbers in this chart form a pattern. Can you figure out what it is? _____

_____

How much would a box of 10 roll-ups weigh? _____

How much would it cost to ship? _____

How much would a box of 20 roll-ups weigh? _____

How much would it cost to ship? _____

(continued)

Professor Percy Palindrome

World-Famous Scientist, Inventor Extraordinaire (and Lawns Mowed)

Of course, when people get a taste of that exquisite squid flavor, they'll want more. Here's a shipping chart for the larger 6-ounce roll-up, the perfect size for a hearty breakfast!

Number of Roll-Ups	Weight (in ounces)	Shipping Cost
1	6	$3
2	12	$6
3	18	$9
4	24	$12
5	30	$15

This chart also forms a pattern. Can you figure out what it is? _____

_____

How much would a box of 10 roll-ups weigh? _____

How much would it cost to ship? _____

Sincerely,

Professor Percy Palindrome

Name: _____ Date: _____

Raquel wants to buy 1-foot-square corkboard squares to cover one wall in her room. What formula could she use to figure out how many corkboard squares she needs? If her wall is 8 feet high and 10 feet long, how many corkboard squares would she need?

BASICS BOX

Expression – A way to show a number or quantities. It includes numbers, operations, and, at times, variables. For example, 4 + 7 and 3 x Y are expressions.

Formula – Shows a rule with symbols and includes an equal sign. Area = Length x Width is a formula. A = L x W is another way to write the same formula.

For Raquel, if she knows Area = Length x Width or A = L x W, she could plug in the 8' for L and 10' for W, multiply, and find an area of 80 square feet. She needs 80 corkboard squares.

PRACTICE

Although Professor Palindrome hasn't received a single Squid Roll-Ups order, he has ordered Hibbins to design a package for the product. Hibbins has decided to try several different-size packages. In addition, Hibbins weighed the packages so he could calculate their shipping costs. Review the chart at right, fill in the blanks, and answer the questions below:

Experiment #1	
Number of Squid Roll-Ups	**Weight (in ounces)**
1	10
2	
	30
4	
5	50

1. What is the rule that tells what a package of roll-ups will weigh if you know the number of roll-ups in the package? _____

2. Circle the expression that shows the weight of the package if you know the number of roll-ups:

   5 x N   6 x N   10 x N

3. Circle the formula that shows the weight of the package if you know the number of roll-ups:

   Weight = 5 x N   Weight = 6 x N   Weight = 10 x N

(continued)

Name: _____ Date: _____

Experiment #2	
Number of Squid Roll-Ups	**Weight (in ounces)**
1	
2	14
	21
	28
5	

4. For experiment #2, what is the rule that tells what a package of roll-ups will weigh if you know the number of roll-ups in the package?

   _____

5. Write the expression that shows the weight of the package if you know the number of roll-ups.

   _____

6. Write the formula that shows the weight of the package if you know the number of roll-ups. _____

Experiment #3			
Number of Squid Roll-Ups	**Weight of Roll-Ups (in ounces)**	**Weight of the Prize (in ounces)**	**Total Weight (in ounces)**
1	20	3	23
2	40	3	43
	60	3	63
4			83
5			

Hibbins decided to add a prize to each package to make people want to buy them. (The prize was a Hibbins action figure.) Each prize weighs 3 ounces.

7. What is the rule that tells the weight of a package of roll-ups if you know the number of roll-ups in the package? _____

8. Circle the expression that tells the weight of the package if you know the number of roll-ups:

   $15 \times N + 3$ $16 \times N + 3$ $20 \times N + 3$

9. Circle the formula that tells the weight of the package if you know the number of roll-ups:

   Weight = $15 \times N + 3$ Weight = $16 \times N + 3$ Weight = $20 \times N + 3$

JOURNAL

Could you use the letter Y instead of the letter N in the formula for weight of a package of Squid Roll-Ups? Why or why not?

Reteaching Math: Algebra Readiness © 2008 by Bob Krech, Scholastic Teaching Resources

Name: _____   Date: _____

Expressions and Formulas

1. Out = 2 x In + 1

Fill in the In/Out table using this formula
if In = 1, 2, 3, 4, 5

In	Out
1	
2	
3	
4	
5	

2. Out = 5 x In + 3

Fill in the In/Out table using this formula
if In = 1, 2, 3, 4, 5

In	Out
1	
2	
3	
4	
5	

3. Circle the correct formula:

In	Out
1	7
2	14
3	21
4	28
5	35

a. Out = 5 × In + 2

b. Out = In + 6

c. Out = In × 7

d. Out = In ÷ 7

4. Circle the correct formula:

In	Out
1	7
2	12
3	17
4	22
5	27

a. Out = 5 × In + 2

b. Out = In + 6

c. Out = In × 7

d. Out = In ÷ 7

(continued)

Name: _____   Date: _____

Expressions and Formulas

5. Circle the correct formula:

In	Out
1	7
2	8
3	9
4	10
5	11

a. Out = 5 × In + 2

b. Out = In + 6

c. Out = In × 7

d. Out = In ÷ 7

6. Circle the expression(s):

a. X + 3

b. 7 + 2 = 9

c. 7N − 1

7. Circle the formula(s):

a. 2y × 4 = 20

b. V = L × W × H

c. 4 − 2N

Review:

8. D, C, A, B, D, C, A, B, D, C . . .

What is the core of this pattern? _____

9. 2, 5, 8, 11, 14, 17 . . .

What is the start number? _____   What is the jump number? _____

Reteaching Math: Algebra Readiness © 2008 by Bob Krech, Scholastic Teaching Resources

Professor Percy Palindrome

World-Famous Scientist, Inventor Extraordinaire (and Lawns Mowed)

Greetings, Young Scientists and Mathematicians!

I am proud to announce that Squid Roll-Ups are a success. We are selling huge numbers of roll-ups to the fine people of the island nation of Notaste Atoll. It's only a matter of time before the rest of the world hops on the Squid Roll-Ups bandwagon!

Here are our sales to Notaste Atoll for the first five weeks:

Sales of Squid Roll-Ups Sales Territory: Notaste Atoll	
Week Number	**Roll-Ups Sold**
1	2
2	4
3	6
4	8
5	10

What is the rule for this pattern? _____

What is the formula for this pattern? _____

How many roll-ups do you think we will sell in week 10? _____

On the grid at right, draw a line graph that shows how many Squid Roll-Ups we sold in the first five weeks.

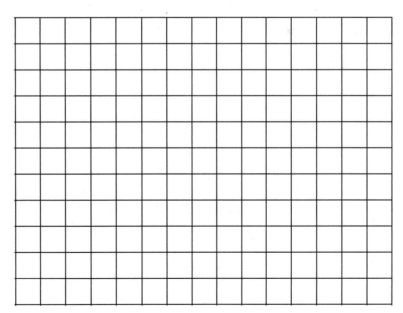

Sincerely,

Professor Percy Palindrome

Reteaching Math: Algebra Readiness © 2008 by Bob Krech, Scholastic Teaching Resources

Name: _____ Date: _____

Make-a-Graph Swap and Match

Directions:

Fill in the table with data you created. (For example, you might record how many pages of your book you read each day for five days.) Then plot this data on the graph below. When you're finished, cut along the dashed line and give both sides to your teacher for a swap-and-match activity.

Table

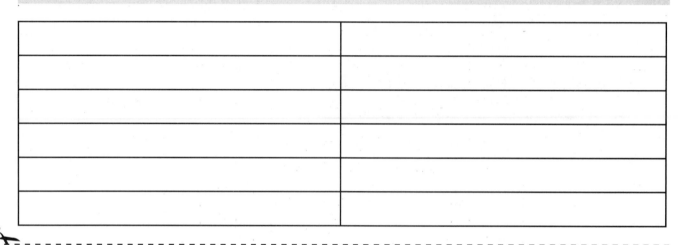

✂ —

Graph

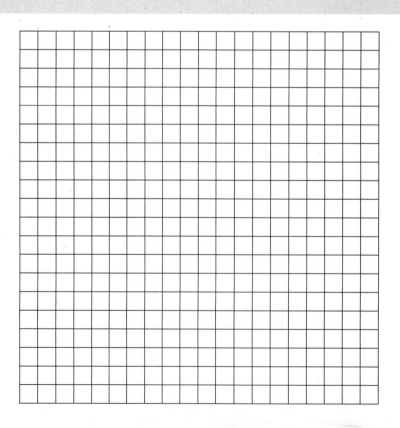

Reteaching Math: Algebra Readiness © 2008 by Bob Krech, Scholastic Teaching Resources

Name: _____   Date: _____

Melanie decided to start saving money. On the first day, she saved 2 cents and plans to save 2 cents more each day afterward. What is the formula to calculate how much she saved on a particular day? How much would she save on Day 10? Draw a graph to show this.

BASICS BOX

If you know the formula for a pattern, you can use it to create a line graph. The formula that shows how much Melanie saved on a particular day is Amount Saved = 2 x Day Number. On Day 1, she saved 2 cents. By Day 10, she would have saved 20 cents.

To create a graph, use the formula to write out the ordered pairs. (Generally, it's best to use the horizontal or x-axis for time.) Some ordered pairs would be (1, 2), (2, 4), (5, 10), and (7, 14). Plot these points to complete the graph. Consider extending the line to show how much she saved after the tenth week.

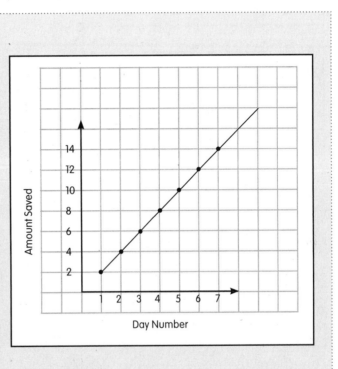

PRACTICE

The people of the tiny nation of Notaste Atoll can't get enough Squid Roll-Ups! The success has the professor in a frenzy. "Hibbins!" he bellowed. "I must have those sales figures immediately. And don't forget to add those splendid graphs. They are so informative!" Look at the graphs Hibbins prepared and answer the questions.

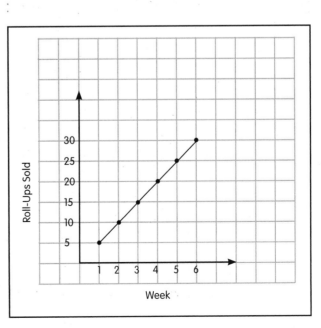

Reteaching Math: Algebra Readiness © 2008 by Bob Krech, Scholastic Teaching Resources

(continued)

Name: _____ Date: _____

1. Complete the table, showing how many roll-ups were sold in the first six weeks.

In/Out Table	
Week Number	Roll-Ups Sold
1	
2	
3	
4	
5	
6	

6. Complete the table, showing how many roll-ups were sold in the next six weeks.

In/Out Table	
Week Number	Roll-Ups Sold
7	
8	
9	
10	
11	
12	

2. How many roll-ups were sold in week 5? _____

3. What is the ordered pair that shows the number of roll-ups sold in week 4? _____

4. What is the formula for this pattern? _____

7. How many roll-ups were sold in week 9? _____

8. What is the ordered pair that shows the number of roll-ups sold in week 11? _____

9. What is the formula for this pattern? _____

5. Predict what the sales will be for weeks 7 through 12 and complete the graph at right:

JOURNAL

Do you think Professor Palindrome should expect that the increase in sales for the first six weeks will continue? Why or why not?

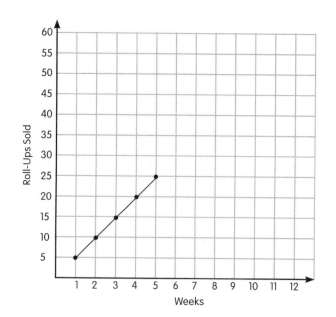

Reteaching Math: Algebra Readiness © 2008 by Bob Krech, Scholastic Teaching Resources

Name: _____   Date: _____

Graphing Functional Relationships

For each formula, fill in the In/Out table using the formula if In = 1, 2, 3, 4, 5.
Graph the data from your table.

1. Out = 5 x In

In	1	2	3	4	5
Out					

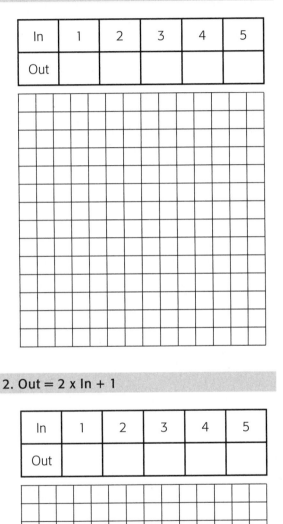

3. Out = 2 x In − 2

In	1	2	3	4	5
Out					

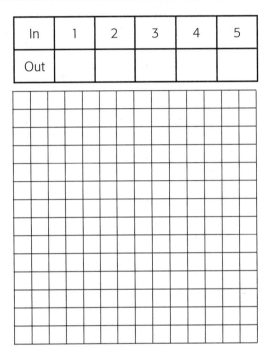

2. Out = 2 x In + 1

In	1	2	3	4	5
Out					

4. Out = 5 x In − 3

In	1	2	3	4	5
Out					

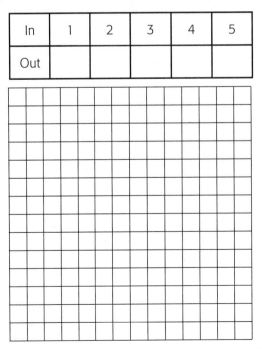

Reteaching Math: Algebra Readiness © 2008 by Bob Krech, Scholastic Teaching Resources

From the Desk of Hibbins

Loyal Assistant to Professor Percy Palindrome

My Dear Young Scientists and Mathematicians:

Sales of Squid Roll-Ups to Notaste Atoll have been very fine indeed, but we need to have a more attractive package. So I'm asking you to create a drawing or diagram that will be part of the design of the new package. Since we love mathematics and science, I've decided that the design will have a mathematical theme. Did you know that a squid has 10 tentacles? I would like your drawing or diagram to show the solution to the following problem:

If 12 squid were swimming together, how many tentacles are there in all?

Your drawing or diagram should show how you arrived at the answer. You may use symbols if you wish.

Sincerely,

Hibbins

Reteaching Math: Algebra Readiness © 2008 by Bob Krech, Scholastic Teaching Resources

Name: _____   Date: _____

My Wonderful Product

Name of Product: _____

Describe Product: _____

Directions: Draw a picture or diagram of the front of a package for your product. The picture should show how many of the items are in the package. The picture should also represent a pattern. Include a formula to match the picture of the pattern.

Pattern: _____

Formula: _____

Name: _____   Date: _____

Fernando formed a ring of fruits around a cake he baked. He put the fruits in a pattern of cherry, cherry, strawberry, blueberry, starting again with cherry. When he had finished, he had used 10 cherries. How many blueberries did he use?

BASICS BOX

Sometimes when you're having a hard time figuring out how to solve a word problem, making a drawing or diagram can help. Drawings and diagrams can also help you see patterns and can give you ideas on what steps to take to solve a problem. There is no one correct way to make a drawing or diagram. You can use symbols or other elements. Try different approaches and use the method that works best for you.

If we drew Fernando's ring, this is what it might look like:

As you can see, if Fernando used 10 cherries, then he must have used 5 blueberries.

PRACTICE

Sales of Squid Roll-Ups to Notaste Atoll have been so good that Hibbins needs his own assistant to help him keep up with the orders. He immediately hired Griselda, the only one who applied for the job. As Hibbins started training her, he realized that she was from another planet and couldn't speak or read English. Hibbins had to find another way to teach Griselda how to make Squid Roll-Ups. He decided to use pictures and diagrams instead of words.

Super-Secret Recipe for Squid Roll-Ups:
• 2 medium-size squid
• 1 glue stick

1. Mix the ingredients in a food processor.

2. Pour the mixture into a hot pan and fry until bubbling.

3. Pour the heated mixture onto a cookie sheet.

4. Put into the freezer for one hour.

Makes one large (10-ounce) Squid Roll-Up.

(continued)

Reteaching Math: Algebra Readiness © 2008 by Bob Krech, Scholastic Teaching Resources

Name: _____   Date: _____

1. Pretend you are Hibbins. Make a drawing or diagram to show Griselda what ingredients she needs to mix together for a batch of 5 roll-ups.

2. Griselda did a great job with the first batch of roll-ups. Hibbins has decided that she is ready to make a larger batch of 20 large roll-ups. Make a drawing or diagram for Griselda to follow to make 20 large roll-ups.

JOURNAL

What quantities do you think are needed to make a ridiculously large (40-ounce) Squid Roll-up? How did you get your answer?

Name: _____   Date: _____

Drawings, Diagrams, and Patterns

1. Gwen has a job walking dogs in the neighborhood. She makes $2 for every dog she walks. This picture shows how much money she would make if she walked 5 dogs.

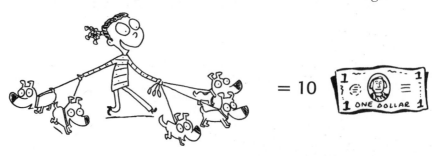

Gwen hopes to start walking more dogs to earn more money. Complete the In/Out table to help her figure out how much more money she could earn.

In/Out Table	
Dogs Walked	**Amount Earned**
5	$10
10	
15	
20	
25	

2. Shannon likes to buy crayons from the Slightly Used Crayon Store. The crayons are very cheap, but each box that originally held 8 crayons is missing 1. Shannon has devised a formula to calculate the total number of crayons she will have if she buys N boxes of crayons:

Total Crayons = N × (8 − 1)

Does Shannon's formula work? Why or why not? Complete the In/Out table.

In/Out Table	
Crayon Boxes	**Total**
1	
2	
3	
4	

(continued)

Reteaching Math: Algebra Readiness © 2008 by Bob Krech, Scholastic Teaching Resources

Name: _____   Date: _____

Drawings, Diagrams, and Patterns

Make a drawing to show how many crayons Shannon will end up with if she buys 7 boxes.

```




```

3. Bella likes to collect Smelly Animal cards. They come in packs of 8. Because she is a good sister, Bella gives half the cards from each pack she buys to her sister Clara. So if she buys 2 packs, she starts out with 16 then gives half to Clara and keeps half. Complete the In/Out table.

Bella has determined that the formula to calculate the number of cards she gets to keep when she buys N packs is Cards Kept = N + 3. Is she correct? Why or why not? _____

_____

In/Out Table	
Packs Bought	**Number of Cards Bella Keeps**
1	
2	
3	
4	
5	

Draw a picture showing what happens when Bella buys 6 packs of cards.

```




```

From the Desk of Hibbins

Loyal Assistant to Professor Percy Palindrome

My Dear Young Scientists and Mathematicians:

Griselda has been working very hard and has been doing a first-class job as my loyal assistant. I've been thinking of letting her do more work on her own now that she can speak and read English, but I'm not sure if she's ready. I thought of giving her a kind of test—a set of problems to work on so I can see how much she really understands. Here are some of the problems I've been thinking about giving her. Please try them out.

1. Adam has 3 boxes of toad diapers. He has 27 diapers in all. How many toad diapers are in each box? Write this problem as a formula with an "unknown."

2. Mandy has twice as many cans of anchovies as Penny. Mandy has 46 cans. How many cans does Penny have? Write this as a formula with an unknown.

3. Trish had 4 packs of salamander sausage and 2 loose sausages. She has 22 sausages in all. How many sausages are in a pack? Write this as a formula with an unknown.

4. Write a story problem for the formula $24 \div X = 8$.

Sincerely,

Hibbins

Reteaching Math: Algebra Readiness © 2008 by Bob Krech, Scholastic Teaching Resources

Name: _____ Date: _____

How Often Do I . . . ?

Directions: Choose an activity that you do more than once a day, such as brushing your teeth. Fill in the blanks below to figure out how often you do this activity in one day, one week, one month, one year, and so on.

Activity: _____

Draw a picture of your activity here.

---

1 Day

How often in 1 day? _____

N = Number of times activity is done in 1 day

N = _____

Formula for 1 day: _____

Solve: _____

1 Week

Formula for 1 week: _____

Solve: _____

1 Month

Formula for 1 month: _____

Solve: _____

1 Year

Formula for 1 year: _____

Solve: _____

10 Years

Formula for 10 years: _____

Solve: _____

100 Years

Formula for 100 years: _____

Solve: _____

Reteaching Math: Algebra Readiness © 2008 by Bob Krech, Scholastic Teaching Resources

Name: _____ Date: _____

Carmela makes 12 cookies every hour. If she bakes for 3 hours, how many cookies will she make in all? Write this problem as a formula with a variable and then solve.

BASICS BOX

Variable — Symbols or letters that represent unknown amounts. To figure out what quantity a variable stands for, you can try the "guess and check" strategy. You should also keep fact families in mind, and remember that addition is the opposite of subtraction and multiplication is the opposite of division. Sometimes, turning an addition problem into a subtraction problem can help.

We could write about Carmela's situation using N to stand for the number of hours she is baking because this number varies. The number of cookies she makes per hour is always the same—it's constant. So, she could write:

Total Cookies = 12 x N

with N being the number of hours baking. If we plug 3 in for N, we find the answer is 36 cookies.

PRACTICE

Griselda has proven herself to be an excellent worker as well as a loyal assistant. She has even learned to read English. Hibbins isn't quite sure if she is ready to work on her own, so he has prepared a short but challenging test for her. If she passes, she will be promoted to Senior Loyal Assistant to the Loyal Assistant. Can you pass the test yourself?

1. In each equation, what is the value of X?

   a. $10 + X = 14$

   b. $7 \times 4 = X$

   c. $21/X = 7$

   d. $(7 + X) \times 2 = 20$

2. Professor Palindrome created 8 incredibly smelly slugs in his laboratory. Unfortunately, 6 escaped into the surrounding community. How many incredibly smelly slugs did he have left? Circle the equation that best fits the problem.

   a. $8 + 6 = X$

   b. $8 \times 6 = X$

   c. $8 - 6 = X$

(continued)

Name: _____ Date: _____

3. Professor Palindrome developed an automatic toenail clipper. On Tuesday, he tested it out on 8 volunteers. On Wednesday, he tested it on more volunteers. In all, 24 volunteers had their toenails clipped. How many were tested on Wednesday? Circle the equation that best fits the story.

    a. 24/8 = X

    b. 8 + X = 24

    c. 24 + 8 = X

4. Professor Palindrome has twice as many sticks of broccoli gum (another great invention!) as Hibbins. If Professor Palindrome has 50 sticks, how many does Hibbins have? Circle the equation that best fits the story.

    a. 2 × 50 = X

    b. 2 × X = 50

    c. 50 × 2 = X

5. Write an equation that fits the story:

    Professor Palindrome developed a weed-eating warthog he named Portia. Unfortunately Portia also loves to eat every living plant in the garden! Once, he had 100 flowers in his garden. After Portia visited his garden, he had only 5 left. How many did Portia eat?

    JOURNAL

    Erica and Ben were asked to write an equation for this story: I want to buy 35 hot dogs. Hot dogs come 7 to a package. How many packages do I need to buy? Erica wrote 7 x N = 35. Ben wrote 35/7 = N. Who is right? Why?

Name: _____   Date: _____

Variables

Find the value of X:

1. $19 - X = 12$

2. $X \times 13 = 52$

3. $28 \div X = 14$

4. $2X \div 5 = 8$

5. $X = 3 + 2 \times 7$

6. $10 \div (X + 2) = 2$

7. $X \times 5 = 35$

8. $7 + X = 20$

9. $X + 2 \times 5 = 14$

10. $X = 7 + 13$

11. $9 \times X = 81$

12. $X \times (3 + 2) = 55$

Circle the equation that best fits the story.

13. Amanda ate 3 slices of anchovy pizza. Vineet ate 4 slices. If the pie started out with 8 slices, how many are left?
    a. $X = 3 + 4$
    b. $X = 8 - (3 + 4)$
    c. $X = 8 - 3 + 4$

14. Grace bought 7 Larry Potter trading cards on Monday, some more on Tuesday, and 12 more on Wednesday. In all, she bought 25. How many did she buy on Tuesday?
    a. $X = 25 - (7 + 12)$
    b. $X + 8 + 25 = 12$
    c. $X = 25 - 7 + 12$

15. Pavel went to his favorite store, Bad Breath and Beyond. He bought 7 cases of mouthwash on Monday and 8 cases on Tuesday. Each case holds 8 bottles. How many did he buy in all?
    a. $8 \times 7 \times 8 = X$
    b. $8 + 7 \times 8 = X$
    c. $X = (8 + 7) \times 8$

16. Lizzie split her bottle cap collection evenly with Megan and Daniel. If she started with 39 bottle caps, how many did each person receive?
    a. $X = 3 \times 13$
    b. $X = 39 \div 13$
    c. $X = 39 \div 3$

17. Sohan and Katie planted 10 plants. Two were eaten by rabbits. Each surviving plant had 7 flowers. How many flowers were there in all? Write this as an equation with a variable. _____

Review:

18. What will the In number be if the Out number is 70? _____

In	Out
1	7
2	14
3	21
4	28
5	35

From the Desk of Griselda

Senior Loyal Assistant to the Loyal Assistant

Hey Science and Math Dudes!

My name is Griselda. I believe you have heard about me from my most excellent mentor, Hibbins, and that groovy cat, Professor Palindrome. I'm from that planet the professor was contacting way back, but now that I've learned English I'm grooving here on Earth. Working in the Secret Lab is totally awesome!

The sale of Squid Roll-Ups to Notaste Atoll has been most triumphant! We are almost out of the Ridiculously Large size (40 ounces). We have some of the Extra-Large size (20 ounces), and lots of the Large size (10 ounces). Professor P just received an order for 20 Ridiculously Large roll-ups but we have only 10 in the lab. This was a problem!

I immediately said, "Excuse me, dudes, but I have been weighing squid every day on the scale and I know that one 20-ounce roll-up weighs the same as two 10-ounce roll-ups. Why don't we just substitute Large and Extra-Large roll-ups that have the same weight as the order for the Ridiculously Large ones?"

The Professor and Hibbins shouted, "Brilliant!" As you can see, I ended up fixing a lot of the orders. Check out my work and see whether or not I'm correct.

Remember: To keep a balancing scale in balance, the weight on one arm must be the same as the weight on the other. Equations must also balance. The amount on one side of the equal sign must be the same as the amount on the other. The equal sign means "the same as."

Squid Roll-Ups Size Chart			
Size	Large	Extra-Large	Ridiculously Large
Weight	10 oz	20 oz	40 oz

1. Is my substitution correct? _____

   Why or why not? _____

Order
2 ridiculously large roll-ups

Substitution
2 extra-large and 4 large roll-ups

Reteaching Math: Algebra Readiness © 2008 by Bob Krech, Scholastic Teaching Resources

(continued) **79**

From the Desk of Griselda

Senior Loyal Assistant to the Loyal Assistant

2.

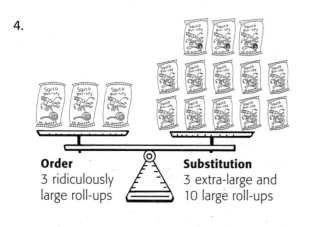

Order
5 ridiculously
large roll-ups

Substitution
6 extra-large and
8 large roll-ups

Is my substitution correct? Why or why not?

_____

3.

Order
4 ridiculously
large roll-ups

Substitution
8 large roll-ups

Is my substitution correct? Why or why not?

_____

On my day off, Professor Palindrome decided to fill the orders himself—not one of his better ideas. Look at what the Professor did with these orders and decide if he shipped the customer greater than, less than, or equal to the amount they ordered.

4.

Order
3 ridiculously
large roll-ups

Substitution
3 extra-large and
10 large roll-ups

Is the substitution greater than, less than, or equal to the order? How do you know?

_____

5.

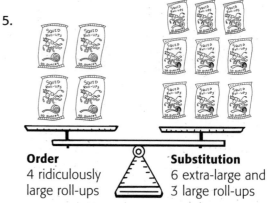

Order
4 ridiculously
large roll-ups

Substitution
6 extra-large and
3 large roll-ups

Is the substitution greater than, less than, or equal to the order? How do you know?

_____

Sincerely,

Griselda

Reteaching Math: Algebra Readiness © 2008 by Bob Krech, Scholastic Teaching Resources

Name: _____ Date: _____

Balance Scale Drawings

Directions: For the first two problems, use the key below to draw pictures that show balanced equations. Then write the equation on the line.

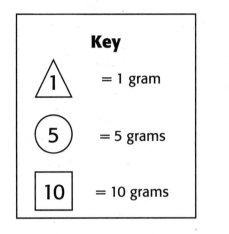

Key

△ 1 = 1 gram

○ 5 = 5 grams

□ 10 = 10 grams

3. Draw a picture showing a balanced equation and write the equation on the line. Use your own key and symbols.

Your Key

1.

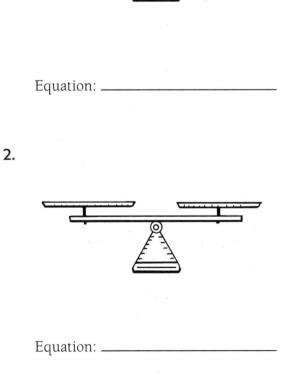

Equation: _____

2.

Equation: _____

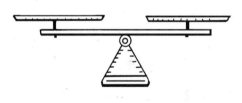

Equation: _____

Name: _____ Date: _____

WORD PROBLEM

The Tornado Triplets were playing on a seesaw in the park. They were joined by the Turkowski Twins, the Tully Twins, and the Tang Triplets. All of the kids weigh about the same size. How should they arrange themselves on the seesaw so that it is balanced? Write your solution as an equation.

BASICS BOX

The symbols >, <, and = can be used in place of the words *greater than*, *less than*, and *equal to*. Some people think that the equal sign means "find the answer," but it actually means "the same as." Think of the equal sign as the middle of a balancing scale. What is on one side of the equal sign must be the same as what is on the other side.

Since there are 10 children all together, one pair of triplets and one set of twins should get on each side of the seesaw. This would put 5 on each side and the seesaw would then be balanced. It could be written as:
Tornado + Tornado + Tornado + Tully + Tully = Tang + Tang + Tang + Turkowski + Turkowski

PRACTICE

Griselda created these stimulating mental puzzles to amuse Professor Palindrome, who was feeling a bit bored. See if you can solve them. Fill in the missing information on the balancing scales.

1.

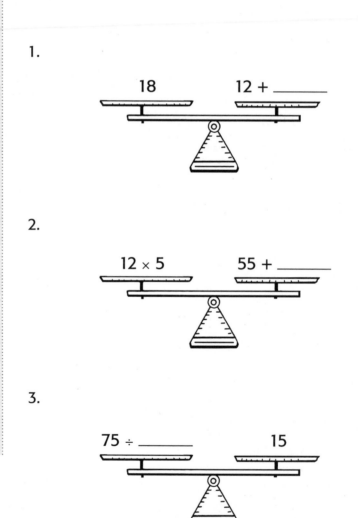

18 $12 +$ _____

2.

12×5 $55 +$ _____

3.

$75 \div$ _____ 15

(continued)

Reteaching Math: Algebra Readiness © 2008 by Bob Krech, Scholastic Teaching Resources

Name: _____   Date: _____

Write the amount that belongs in each shape.

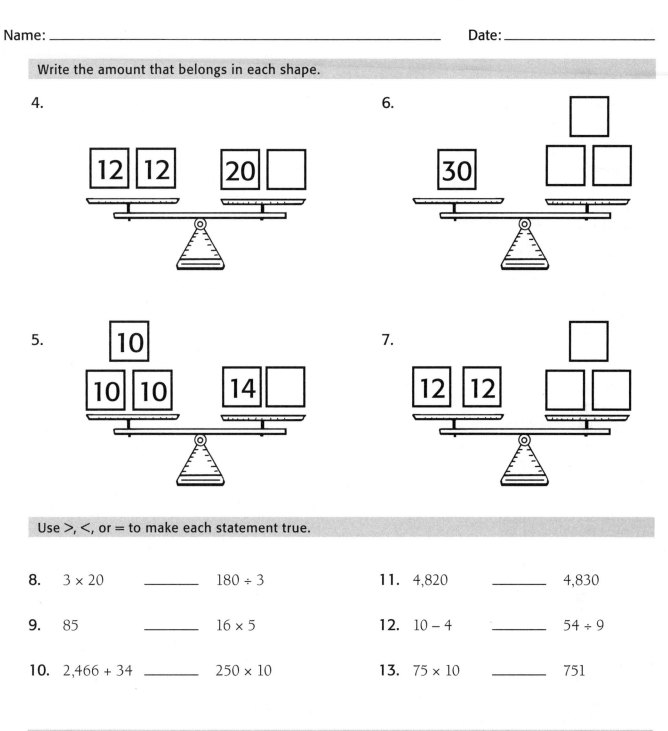

4.

5.

6.

7.

Use >, <, or = to make each statement true.

8. 3×20 _____ $180 \div 3$

9. 85 _____ 16×5

10. $2,466 + 34$ _____ 250×10

11. 4,820 _____ 4,830

12. $10 - 4$ _____ $54 \div 9$

13. 75×10 _____ 751

JOURNAL

Based on the drawing of the balancing scale, which weighs more—the circle or the triangle? How do you know?

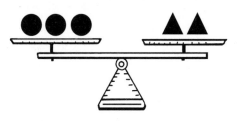

Name: _____ Date: _____

Balancing Equations

Fill in the missing information to keep the scale balanced.

Left Arm of Balance	Right Arm of Balance

1. 27   54 ÷ _____

2. 81 ÷ 9   17 − _____

3. 4 × (3 + _____)   36

4. 13 × 2 + 2   _____ × 7

5. 64 ÷ 16   40 ÷ _____

Write the amount that belongs in each shape to keep the scale balanced.

Left Arm of Balance	Right Arm of Balance

6. ☐ ☐ ☐ ☐   36

7. 7 7 7   20 ☐

8. ☐ ☐ ☐   14 4

9. 30   ☐ ☐ ☐ ☐ ☐

10. 19   1 ☐ ☐ ☐

Use >, <, or = to make each statement true.

11. 16 × 5 _____ 150 ÷ 2   15. 1,977 _____ 999 × 2

12. 57 _____ 3 × 19   16. 100 _____ 11 × 9

13. 847 _____ 84 × 10   17. 700 + 50 _____ 150 × 5

14. 1,000 ÷ 100 _____ 10 × 10   18. 804 + 40 _____ 8,044

Review:

19. Circle the expression that best fits the problem:

The Full-Contact Hopscotch League has 8 teams. At the beginning of each season, each team was given 10 pieces of chalk. Each team has used 4 pieces. How many pieces of chalk are left?

a. 10 − 8 × 4
b. (10 − 4) × 8
c. 10 − 8 + 4

20. What is the rule for this table?

In	1	2	3	4	5	6
Out	2	9	16	23	30	37

a. Out = In + 1
b. Out = In × 2
c. Out = 7 × In − 5

Reteaching Math: Algebra Readiness © 2008 by Bob Krech, Scholastic Teaching Resources

From the Desk of Griselda

Senior Loyal Assistant to the Loyal Assistant

Hey, Science and Math Dudes!

Things have been most excellent here in the lab! Professor Palindrome is brilliant, but not always mathematically precise.

Yesterday, he got most perplexed over my reorganizing the shelves that hold the solar-powered tongue depressors. We have 50 of them. He used to keep 10 of them crammed on 5 small shelves. Now I have 5 each on 10 shelves, and I think they're much easier to reach. Professor Palindrome says he now has fewer solar-powered tongue depressors. I say we have the same number. Which one of us is correct? Why?

_____

_____

_____

The other day I was working on my first invention—a pollution-free, inexpensive fusion reactor. On the morning of the first day, it produced enough energy to light 25 homes. In the afternoon, it produced enough energy to light 15 homes. The next day, it produced enough for 15 homes in the morning and 25 homes in the afternoon. Professor Palindrome said it's too bad that the reactor did better the first day than the second. I thought it produced the same amount of energy both days. Which one of us is correct? Why?

_____

_____

_____

Sincerely,

Griselda

Reteaching Math: Algebra Readiness © 2008 by Bob Krech, Scholastic Teaching Resources

Name: _____ Date: _____

Reteaching Math: Algebra Readiness © 2008 by Bob Krech, Scholastic Teaching Resources

WORD PROBLEM

In Gino's first week as a paperboy he earned $5 a day for every day he worked. He worked 7 days that week. The second week he could work only 5 days, but he earned $7 each day. In which week did he earn more money?

BASICS BOX

Commutative Property of Addition – In an addition problem, the order of the addends can be switched without changing the sum. For example, 6 + 7 = 7 + 6. To show this rule works for all numbers, we can say that a + b = b + a.

Commutative Property of Multiplication – In a multiplication problem, the order of the factors can be switched without changing the product. For example, 4 x 5 = 5 x 4. To show that this rule works for all numbers, we can say that a x b = b x a.

In Gino's problem we can see that he earned $35 the first week ($5 x 7). In the second week we see he earned the same amount because $7 x 5 = $35. The commutative property of multiplication works here because 5 x 7 = 7 x 5.

PRACTICE

After a great deal of thought, Professor Palindrome has turned his attention to raising giant mushrooms for people to keep as pets. He has ordered supplies needed for his research. Hibbins and Griselda have just finished opening the supply packages when they notice the professor looking upset. Help Hibbins and Griselda calm the professor down.

1. Professor Palindrome noticed that he received a delivery of 37 bags of fertilizer, then a second delivery of 53 bags. "But I ordered 53 bags in my first order and 37 in my second," he wailed. "Now I don't have the right amount to work with. This is a total disaster!" What should Hibbins and Griselda tell Professor Palindrome?

   _____

   _____

2. Professor Palindrome looks at the bill from the Adams Supply Company. "It says I bought 90 mushroom leashes that cost 27 cents each. This is an outrage! The bill should say I paid 27 cents for 90 leashes. If the 27 comes first when I multiply, I'll owe them less money." What should Hibbins and Griselda tell the professor?

   _____

   _____

JOURNAL

Would you rather have a box of candy that is arranged in 6 rows with 7 pieces per row, or one arranged in 7 rows with 6 pieces per row? Explain your answer.

Name: _____ Date: _____

Commutative Property of Addition and Multiplication

Fill in the blanks, then find the sum.

1. $8 + 10 + 12 =$ _____ $+ 12 + 8 =$ _____

2. $33n + 7n + 60n = 7n +$ _____ $+$ _____ $=$ _____

3. $3 + 4 + 7 + 6 =$ _____ $+ 3 +$ _____ $+ 6 =$ _____

4. $19n + 11n + 4n + 16n =$ _____ $+ 16n +$ _____ $+ 11n =$ _____

Fill in the blanks, then find the product.

5. $7 \times 9 = 9 \times$ _____ $=$ _____

6. $5n \times 6n = 6n \times$ _____ $=$ _____

7. $2 \times 5 \times 10 =$ _____ $\times$ _____ $\times 2 =$ _____

8. $4 \times 5 \times 3 = 5 \times$ _____ $\times$ _____ $=$ _____

Review:

9. Find the value of X in each equation:

  a. $X - 17 = 24$

  b. $2X + 1 = 15$

  c. $21 - 2X = 5$

  d. $4X - 7 = 33$

  e. $32 \div X = 4$

  f. $(X - 7) \times 3 = 9$

10. Use >, <, or = to make each statement true.

  a. 15×6 _____ 8×11

  b. $90 - 7$ _____ 7×12

  c. $48 \div 12$ _____ $82 - 78$

  d. $7,047$ _____ $5,247 + 1,801$

  e. 10×12 _____ 40×3

From the Desk of Griselda

Senior Loyal Assistant to the Loyal Assistant

Hey, Science and Math Dudes!

The other day, Professor P called Hibbins and me into his private office. "My loyal assistants," he began. "I have decided to enter the Federal Office of Learning competition. The FOOL award will be the crowning achievement of my career and will provide the funds we need to keep making secret discoveries."

The professor continued, "We need to make sure our laboratory meets all the requirements of the competition. Griselda, make sure that we are using all the latest laws of mathematics and science in our work."

I did some research into the groovy rules of mathematics and I found some wicked cool things we need to put into place in the lab, and pronto. Here's what I found:

Associative Property of Addition

As long as an addition problem involves only addition, the addends can be placed in any order. So, suppose Hibbins ships 7 boxes of Squid Roll-Ups on Wednesday, 6 on Thursday, and 3 on Friday. To find out how many he shipped in all, he could add 7 + 6 + 3 to get 16, or he could rearrange the addends and write the problem as 7 + 3 + 6, which still equals 16. Hibbins thinks this is easier because 7 + 3 = 10 and adding 6 more is 16. Isn't that way cool?

So suppose Hibbins ships 17 boxes of roll-ups one day, 12 the next, and 13 the next. How would you arrange the addends to make the addition easy? _____
What is the sum? _____

Associative Property of Multiplication

As long as a multiplication problem involves only multiplication, the factors can be multiplied in any order. So if Professor Palindrome buys 2 boxes of spiders and each box has 5 spiders and he wants to know how many spider legs he has, he could multiply 8 × 2 × 5, which equals 80 legs. But he would probably find it easier to multiply the 2 × 5 first to get 10, then multiply 10 × 8 to get 80.

(continued)

From the Desk of Griselda

Senior Loyal Assistant to the Loyal Assistant

If Professor Palindrome buys 4 cases of squid and each case contains 8 squid, how many tentacles would there be in all? (Remember that a squid has 10 tentacles.) How would you arrange the factors to make the multiplication easy? _____
What is the product? _____

Identity Property of Multiplication

Any number times 1 equals itself. So, if I can fit 12 plutonium prune pitters on a shelf and we have only one full shelf, we would have 12 x 1 = 12 plutonium prune pitters in all.

If I work 365 days a year and have worked in the Secret Lab for one year, how many days have I worked? _____

Zero Property of Multiplication

Any number times 0 equals 0. So if Professor Palindrome charges $100,000 for each lecture he makes at a college, but no colleges hire him, he would have made 0 × $100,000 = 0.

If I worked 90 hours this week and make $0 per hour,
how much money have I made this week? _____

Identity Property of Addition

Any number plus 0 equals itself. So if we sell 80 cases of Squid Roll-ups one week and 0 cases the next week, we would have sold 80 + 0 = 80 cases in all.

If I work no hours on Saturday (my day off) and 16 hours on Sunday, how many hours have I worked in all? _____

Now that we have our mathematics principles in order, I'm sure we'll win the FOOL prize! Thanks for your help, math and science dudes!

Sincerely,

Griselda

Name: _____ Date: _____

Ivan said that 72 + 29 + 31 = 132. Lucilla said that it is easier if you add the 29 and the 31 first, then add the 72. The answer will be the same. Do you agree or disagree? What addition property applies here?

BASICS BOX

Associative Property of Addition
As long as an addition problem involves only addition, the addends can be added in any order.

Associative Property of Multiplication
As long as a multiplication problem involves only multiplication, the factors can be multiplied in any order.

Identity Property of Multiplication
Any number times 1 equals itself.

Identity Property of Addition
Any number plus 0 equals itself.

Lucilla probably added the 29 and 31 first because she saw it was 60, an easy number to add on to. Both answers would be the same because of the associative property of addition.

PRACTICE

Professor Palindrome continues to raise giant mushrooms for pets. Although a brilliant scientist, he needs Hibbins and Griselda to help him out in matters of common sense.

1. Professor Palindrome convinces 7,982 pet stores to sell his giant pet mushrooms. Each store sells no mushrooms. He isn't too upset because, as he tells Hibbins and Griselda, "7,982 times something has to mean lots of sales." What should Hibbins and Griselda tell Professor Palindrome? _____

    _____

2. Professor Palindrome hears that Lady Kristine's Pampered Pets sold 5 giant mushrooms the first day and 0 for each of the next 10 days. He is encouraged by the news. "After all," he tells his assistants, "5 + 0 + 0 + 0 + 0 + 0 + 0 + 0 + 0 + 0 + 0 has to add up to a really big number with all those addends." What should Hibbins and Griselda tell Professor Palindrome? _____

    _____

3. The world's largest pet store chain wants to make a deal with Professor Palindrome. They have 10,000 stores around the world. They promise to sell 1 pet mushroom per store if they get to be the only store selling them. Professor Palindrome is upset. "One sale for each store can't result in very many mushrooms sold." What should Hibbins and Griselda tell Professor Palindrome? _____

    _____

4. One store sold 5 mushrooms per day during a 7-day week. The mushrooms sell for $10. Group the factors at least two different ways and find the product.

JOURNAL

If you were given the problem 1,751 x 5 x 2, in what order would you group the factors. Why?

Reteaching Math: Algebra Readiness © 2008 by Bob Krech, Scholastic Teaching Resources

Name: _____ Date: _____

Other Properties of Addition and Multiplication

Find the product.

1. $2 \times 100 \times 6 =$ _____

2. $5,572 \times 0 =$ _____

3. $6 \times 8 \times 2 =$ _____

4. $1 \times 5,998 =$ _____

5. $10 \times 75 \times 10 =$ _____

6. $5 \times 32 \times 3 =$ _____

7. $8 \times 4 \times 5 =$ _____

8. $595,932 \times 1 =$ _____

9. $4,578 \times 1 \times 0 =$ _____

10. $0 \times 52 =$ _____

11. $1,957 \times 1 =$ _____

12. $10 \times 7 \times 9 =$ _____

13. $932,887 \times 0 =$ _____

14. $50 \times 2 \times 0 =$ _____

Find the sum.

15. $18 + 17 + 22 =$ _____

16. $56 + 0 =$ _____

17. $0 + 832 =$ _____

18. $5 + 7 + 35 =$ _____

19. $3 + 7 + 60 =$ _____

20. $18 + 27 + 73 =$ _____

21. $81 + 7 + 9 =$ _____

22. $52 + 25 + 8 =$ _____

23. If you were asked to multiply $7 \times 5 \times 2 \times 0$, how would you arrange the factors? Explain your answer.

   _____

   _____

Review:

24. Fill in the table for the following function: Out = $2 \times$ In

In	1	2	3	4	5
Out					

25. $15 + 71 = 71 +$ _____

26. $15 \times 10 =$ _____ $\times 15$

Professor Percy Palindrome

World-Famous Scientist, Inventor Extraordinaire

Greetings, Young Scientists and Mathematicians!

I would like to communicate my sincere thanks to you for all your hard work in service to my Secret Lab. I have watched with great interest and admiration as you have mastered the secrets of algebra, secrets that will help you as you continue to grow as mathematicians.

With the success of Squid Roll-Ups and Giant Pet Mushrooms, I am actually making a pretty good living as a world-famous scientist and inventor extraordinaire. I no longer have to mow lawns to supplement my income (as you can plainly see from the heading of my new stationery).

I believe it is time for me to reward Hibbins and Griselda for their help in making the Secret Laboratory a success. I will be promoting them to the newly created jobs of Assistant World-Famous Scientists and Inventors Extraordinaire. Of course, you know what that means. All three of us will be in need of new loyal assistants! As you are aware, there are animal cages to clean, pieces of equipment to polish, and many other exciting responsibilities. There is no pay, but you get all the Squid Roll-Ups you can eat and a chance to be in the company of the greatest scientist of all time . . . me! Are you interested?

Thank you again for your services!

Sincerely,

Professor Percy Palindrome

Reteaching Math: Algebra Readiness © 2008 by Bob Krech, Scholastic Teaching Resources

Practice Page #1 (p. 31)
Recurring patterns and answers will vary.
Journal: Answers will vary.

Review Page #1 (p. 32)
1.
2.
3. A, B, B, A, B, B, A, B
4. B
5. Answers will vary.
6. Answers will vary, but should represent the "A" symbol of the student's pattern
7. A, C, A; 3, 1, 2
8. The patterns are the same. Explanations will vary.

Practice Page #2 (p. 34)
1.
2.

Journal: Answers will vary.

Review Page #2 (p. 35)
1. A, B, C, D, A, B, C, D, A; the 12th element is D.
2. The core is 1, 2, 2, 1; the 14th element is 2.
3. The 11th element is *; the 18th element is !; explanations will vary.
4. A, B, A, C, A, B, A, C, A; the 21st element is A.
5. The 13th element is ☺; the 22nd element is ♪; explanations will vary.
6. △ □ △ ○
7. A, A, B, B, A, A, B, B, A, A

Practice Page #3 (p. 37)
1.
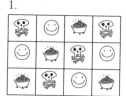

2. ☺

Journal: Answers will vary.

Review Page #3 (p. 38)
1.

A	B	B	A	A
B	B	A	A	B
B	A	A	B	B
A	A	B	B	A
A	B	B	A	A

The sixth row would look like this:

B	B	A	A	B

2.

◇	♡	♡	△	◇	♡
♡	△	◇	♡	♡	△
◇	♡	♡	△	◇	♡
♡	△	◇	♡	♡	△

The sixth row would look like this:

♡	△	◇	♡	♡	△

3.

A	B	A	C	A
B	A	C	A	B
A	C	A	B	A
C	A	B	A	C

If the pattern continued, the 30th element would be B.

4. The patterns are alike because they have a core of ABBA and because they have the same number of elements. They are different because the first grid is four rows of five while the second is five rows of four.
5. A
6. ABBC

Practice Page #4 (p. 40)
1. Add 2 to the previous number
2. Double the previous number
3. Double the amount added each time (+2, +4, +8, +16, etc.)
4. Square numbers (1 × 1, 2 × 2, 3 × 3, etc.)
5. Subtract 4 from the previous number
6. Double the amount added each time (+1, +2, +4, +8, etc.)
7. Subtract one more each time (−1, −2, −3, etc.)
Journal: Answers will vary, but should note that the first pattern is recurring while the second is growing.

Review Page #4 (p. 41)
1. 35, 25, 15
2. 48, 72, 84
3. 2, 3 ½, 4 ½
4. 7, 35, 42
5. 32, 4, 2
6. 8, 17
7. 18, 30, 36
8. 66, 77, 88; add 11
9. 2, ½, ¼; divide by 2
10. 1, 3, 6; recurring pattern
11. A growing pattern does not have a core. Explanations will vary.
12.

5	3	4	2	5	3	4
2	5	3	4	2	5	3
4	2	5	3	4	2	5
3	4	2	5	3	4	2

13. A
14. D

Practice Page #5 (p. 44)

1. Missing numbers: 15 and 23; start number: 3; jump number: 4. Even jump numbers with an odd start number result in an all-odd pattern.
2. Missing numbers: 16 and 26; start number: 1; jump number: 5. Odd jump numbers with an odd start number result in an odd, even, odd, even pattern.
3. Missing number: 22; start number: 2; jump number: 5. Odd jump numbers with an even start number result in an even, odd, even, odd pattern.
4. Missing numbers: 22, 42, and 52; start number: 2; jump number: 10. Even jump numbers with an even start number result in an all-even pattern.

Journal: Answers will vary.

Review Page #5 (p. 45)

1. Start number: 5; jump number: 6
2. Start number: 10; jump number: 4
3. Start number: 4; jump number: 9
4. Start number: 18; jump number: 3
5. 7, 12, 17, 22, 27, 32, 37, 42, 47, 52
6. 3, 13, 23, 33, 43, 53, 63, 73, 83, 93
7. Answers will vary.
8. a. A7B77; b. 7; c. recurring pattern
9. Add 4
10. Add 1 1/2
11. Multiply by 3
12. Subtract 2 1/2

Practice Page #6 (p. 50)

Day Number	1	2	3	4	5	6	7
Cans Made	2	4	6	8	10	12	14

1. 20
2. Double the number of the day to get the number of cans made.
3. Yes, the number of cans made is a function of the day number.

Journal: Answers will vary.

Review Page #6 (p. 51)

1. +11
2. ×2 +1
3. ÷2
4. ×2 −1
5. +2 or ×2
6. Start number: 7; jump number: 3
7. Even

Practice Page #7 (pp. 54–55)

1.

Day Number	Packs Made
1	6
2	10
3	14
4	18
5	22

The rule is to add 4 to the packs made from the previous day, or multiply the day number by 4 and add 2.

2. 42
3. 82
4. Multiply the day by 4 and add 2
5. Add 8 each time
6. 84
7. 164
8. Multiply the day by 8 and add 4

Journal: Answers will vary.

Review Page #7 (p. 56)

1. a. Multiply In by 5; b. 100
2. a. Multiply In by 2 and add 1; b. 21
3. a. Multiply In by 3 and add 3; b. 78
4. a. Multiply In by 5 and subtract 1; b. 124; c. $5 \times In - 1 = Out$

Practice Page #8 (pp. 59–60)

Experiment #1:

Number of Squid Roll-Ups	Weight (in ounces)
1	10
2	20
3	30
4	40
5	50

1. Multiply the number of roll-ups by 10 to get the weight (in ounces)
2. $10 \times N$
3. $Weight = 10 \times N$

Experiment #2:

Number of Squid Roll-Ups	Weight (in ounces)
1	7
2	14
3	21
4	28
5	35

4. Multiply the number of roll-ups by 7 to get the weight (in ounces)
5. $7 \times N$
6. Weight (in ounces) = $7 \times N$

Experiment #3:

Number of Squid Roll-Ups	Weight of Roll-Ups (in ounces)	Weight of the Prize (in ounces)	Total Weight (in ounces)
1	20	3	23
2	40	3	43
3	60	3	63
4	80	3	83
5	100	3	103

7. Multiply the number of roll-ups by 20 and add 3
8. $20 \times N + 3$
9. $Weight = 20 \times N + 3$

Journal: Answers will vary.

Review Page #8 (pp. 61–62)

1.

In	1	2	3	4	5
Out	3	5	7	9	11

2.

In	1	2	3	4	5
Out	8	13	18	23	28

3. c
4. a
5. b
6. a, c
7. a, b
8. DCAB
9. start number: 2; jump number: 3

Practice Page #9 (pp. 65–66)

1.

Week Number	Roll-Ups Sold
1	5
2	10
3	15
4	20
5	25
6	30

2. 25
3. (4, 20)
4. Roll-Ups Sold = Week Number × 5
5.

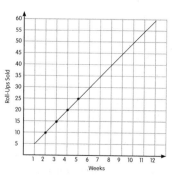

6.

Week Number	Roll-Ups Sold
7	35
8	40
9	45
10	50
11	55
12	60

7. 45
8. (11, 55)
9. Roll-Ups Sold = Week Number × 5
Journal: Answers will vary.

Review Page #9 (p. 67)

1.

In	1	2	3	4	5
Out	5	10	15	20	25

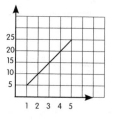

2.

In	1	2	3	4	5
Out	3	5	7	9	11

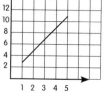

3.

In	1	2	3	4	5
Out	0	2	4	6	8

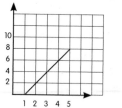

4.

In	1	2	3	4	5
Out	2	7	12	17	22

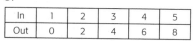

Practice Page #10 (pp. 70–71)

1. Answers will vary, but drawings should show that 10 squid and 5 glue sticks are needed.
2. Answers will vary, but drawings should show that 40 squid and 20 glue sticks are needed.
Journal: Answers will vary.

Review Page #10 (pp. 72–73)

1.

Dogs Walked	Amount Earned
5	$10
10	$20
15	$30
20	$40
25	$50

2.

Crayon Boxes	Total
1	7
2	14
3	21
4	28

95

Shannon's formula works. Explanations will vary.
Student drawings will vary, but should show 7 boxes, each with 7 crayons.

3.

Packs Bought	Cards Bella Keeps
1	4
2	8
3	12
4	16
5	20

The formula N + 3 does not work. While this formula does fit the data for one pack, it doesn't fit additional packs. The correct formula is Cards Kept = N × (8 – 4).
Student drawings will vary, but should show 6 packs of 8 (or 48) divided into 2 groups of 24.

Practice Page #11 (pp. 76–77)
1. a. 4; b. 28; c. 3; d. 3
2. c
3. b
4. b
5. 100 – X = 5 (or 100 – 5 = X)
Journal: Answers will vary.

Review Page #11 (p. 78)

1.	7	10.	20
2.	4	11.	9
3.	2	12.	11
4.	20	13.	b
5.	17	14.	a
6.	3	15.	c
7.	7	16.	c
8.	13	17.	X = 7 × (10 – 2) = 56
9.	4	18.	10

Letter #12 (pp. 79–80)
1. Correct
2. Correct
3. Correct
4. Greater than
5. Less than

Practice Page #12 (pp. 82–83)

1.	6	8.	=
2.	5	9.	>
3.	5	10.	=
4.	4	11.	<
5.	16	12.	=
6.	10, 10, 10	13.	<
7.	8, 8, 8		

Journal: Answers will vary, but should indicate that the triangle weighs more because one triangle equals the weight of 1 1/2 circles.

Review Page #12 (p. 84)

1.	2	11.	>
2.	8	12.	=
3.	6	13.	>
4.	4	14.	<
5.	10	15.	<
6.	9, 9, 9, 9	16.	>
7.	1	17.	=
8.	6, 6, 6	18.	<
9.	6, 6, 6, 6, 6	19.	b
10.	6, 6, 6	20.	c

Practice Page #13 (p. 86)
1. According to the commutative property of addition, 37 + 53 = 53 + 37.
2. According to the commutative property of multiplication, 90 × $0.27 = $0.27 × 90.
Journal: Answers will vary.

Review Page #13 (p. 87)
1. 8 + 10 + 12 = 10 + 12 + 8 = 30
2. 33n + 7n + 60n = 7n + 33n + 60n = 100n
3. 3 + 4 + 7 + 6 = 7 + 3 + 4 + 6 = 20
4. 19n + 11n + 4n + 16n = 4n + 16n + 19n +11n = 50n
5. 7 × 9 = 9 × 7 = 63
6. 5n × 6n = 6n × 5n = 30n
7. 2 × 5 × 10 = 10 × 5 × 2 = 100
8. 4 × 5 × 3 = 5 × 3 × 4 = 60
9. a. 41; b. 7; c. 8; d. 10; e. 8; f. 10
10. a. > b. < c. = d. < e. =

Practice Page #14 (p. 90)
1. Bad news! According to the zero property of multiplication, any number times 0 equals 0. Professor Palindrome hasn't sold any giant mushrooms.
2. More bad news! According to the zero property of addition, any number plus 0 equals that number. Professor Palindrome has sold only 5 mushrooms.
3. Good news! According to the identity property of multiplication, Professor Palindrome will sell at least 10,000 mushrooms.
4. Factor groupings will vary, but the product should always be $350.
Journal: Multiply the 5 × 2 first to get a product of 10, which can easily be used to multiply 1,751.

Review Page #14 (p. 91)

1.	1,200	12.	630
2.	0	13.	0
3.	96	14.	0
4.	5,998	15.	57
5.	7,500	16.	56
6.	480	17.	832
7.	160	18.	47
8.	595,932	19.	70
9.	0	20.	118
10.	0	21.	97
11.	1,957	22.	85

23. Make the 0 the first factor. Anything times 0 equals 0.
24.

In	1	2	3	4	5
Out	2	4	6	8	10

25. 15
26. 10